IT IS
HIS OWN BLOOD

It is His own blood, not the blood of goats and calves, that has enabled Him to enter, once for all, into the sanctuary; the ransom He has won lasts forever.

— Hebrews 9:12

By VINCENT P. McCORRY, S.J.

IT IS
HIS OWN BLOOD

THE BRUCE PUBLISHING COMPANY *Milwaukee*
AMERICA PRESS *New York*

IMPRIMI POTEST:

JOHN J. MCGINTY, S.J., *Provincial*
New York Province, Society of Jesus

NIHIL OBSTAT:

JOHN F. MURPHY, S.T.D.
Censor librorum

IMPRIMATUR:

✠ WILLIAM E. COUSINS
Archbishop of Milwaukee
April 13, 1962

Library of Congress Catalog Card Number: 62–16838

IN MEMORIAM
FATHER LEO T. MARTIN, S.J.

Province of Oregon

*A man so tested and found perfect wins
eternal honor.*

— Ecclesiasticus 31:10

*　　*　　*

With untold thanks to my sister

FLORENCE McCORRY

for immense help with the most tiresome part of the task.

Contents

IT IS
HIS OWN BLOOD

1
Man and God

There is in that philosophical system which is termed Scholastic an axiom that runs: *Contra factum non valet ulla argumentatio:* "Against a fact no amount of argument is of any use." A fairly sensible English novelist of yesterday or the day before contended that the only way to satisfy the average male mind is to give it a fact. Of a highly placed contemporary executive a chastened assistant reported with awe: "When he asks you a question, just give him the facts, and for heaven's sake don't interpret the facts."

It would seem that there is nothing like a fact. A fact is solid, safe, reliable, soothing, satisfying. There it stands, big or little, but always so palpable. You can lean on it or you can hate it, but you can't deny it. It *must* be taken into account.

Well, then. Is God a fact?

No question that can be asked is more precisely vital than that one. Unfortunately, no question is more difficult to answer with total objectivity.

It is evident, of course, that God is not a fact of that order which the philosopher calls sensible, that is, perceptible by any or all of the five human (external) senses. So far as sense perception goes, God is, as St. Paul assured the clever

1

and skeptical Athenians, *the unknown God,* who *does not dwell in temples that our hands have made.* Consequently, Paul continues, *we must not imagine that the divine nature can be represented in gold or silver or stone, carved by man's art and thought.* On the primary, primitive level of the senses, all the biblical talk of seeing God and hearing Him and tasting Him is sheer metaphor.

If anyone wishes to regard this rudimentary divine elusiveness as a difficulty, it yet does not follow that God is in no way an empirical fact.

In the second half of the opening chapter in his Epistle to the Romans, St. Paul has some extremely severe and almost bitter things to say about the pagan world of his day. He sees in the unregenerate pagans *a frame of mind worthy of all scorn, that prompts them to disgraceful acts. They are versed in every kind of injustice, knavery, impurity, avarice, and ill-will; spiteful, murderous, contentious, deceitful, depraved, backbiters, slanderers, God's enemies; insolent, haughty, vainglorious; inventive in wickedness, disobedient to their parents; without prudence, without honor, without love, without loyalty, without pity.* The fierce indictment is breathtaking, but where Paul becomes even more specific he is barely printable.

However, our present interest lies not in Paul's scorching charges, but in the reason which he unhesitatingly assigns for the deplorable moral condition of the men of his time. The root of pagan vice is not viciousness, but ignorance, ignorance of the true God. But the special point is that St. Paul *blames* men for this ignorance; he holds them strictly responsible for it, and therefore culpable in it. Here is his argument:

The knowledge of God is clear to their minds; God Him-

self has made it clear to them; from the foundations of the world men have caught sight of His invisible nature, His eternal power and His divineness, as they are known through His creatures. Thus there is no excuse for them; although they had the knowledge of God, they did not honor Him or give thanks to Him as God; they became fantastic in their notions, and their senseless hearts grew benighted; they, who claimed to be so wise, turned fools, and exchanged the glory of the imperishable God for representations of perishable man, of bird and beast and reptile.

The nerve of this majestic passage is easily exposed. The *invisible nature* of God may and must be *known through His creatures.* When men do not know God thus, *there is no excuse for them.*

So God is mediately and indirectly an empirical fact. Thus St. Paul teaches, and thus, as far as Catholics are concerned, the First Vatican Council has defined.

Setting aside, however, the question of whether men ought to know God by natural evidence, it is indeed a fact, a large and altogether undeniable fact, that any number of men do know God by supernatural revelation. That is to say, whether or not we can in any way know God by our senses, we certainly can and do know Him by faith. The initial article of the Christian Creed is definitive, and it says simply: *I believe in God.*

It is not for any man to reproach his fellowman for lack of supernatural faith, although Christ, in His recorded statements, did not hesitate to blame men for the same. But judgment, as the Savior plainly declares (Jn. 5), belongs to Christ and to no other. Any sane man can see that the phenomenon of supernatural faith is a profoundly mysterious business. Let those who possess religious faith rejoice in it and live by it and even strive cordially to share it. But let them not begin to look about, even in desire, for faggots and a stake.

After the question of the *fact* of God there arises necessarily and at once the related question of the *nature* of God. Very well. God is. But what is God like? How is God to be conceived and described, since *we must not imagine that the divine nature can be represented in gold or silver or stone, carved by man's art and thought?*

We will now limit our answer to that large question and propose only and alliteratively that the Christian God is personal, permanent, and perfect.

In order to gain a comprehensive understanding of what is contained in the concept of *person,* we would have to call in the most professional (and communicative) of the professional philosophers. Enough to say that a person is that unique, complete, separate, sensitive, rational, and volitional entity that we see, for example, in a baby as distinct from an elephant or a rhododendron or an Alp. Every human being is a person. Every individual angel, including the fallen angels, is a person. As for God, it can only be said with all reverence that He is brimful of personality, for God the Father is a Person, and God the Son is a Person, and God the Holy Spirit is a Person.

It follows that God is not to be conceived as a featureless force or a circumambient atmosphere or a compelling environment or a conceptual object of belief. God is not some thing at all. He is some One; some One who is simultaneously Three, each One of the Three being a Person. Hence, the relationship between God and man is, in kind and nature, what the telephone people describe by the expression *person-to-person.*

To say that God is *permanent* is only an inferior mode of saying that he is unconditionally eternal; in the catechism formula, "God always was and always will be." There is little use in trying to persuade the human imagination to construct an image of the eternity of God, because the imagination, for all its agility, is an organic faculty and can only operate on material that is finite or limited. The human intellect can, however, take the concept of time with its natural, usual correlatives of beginning and end, knock out, so to speak, both ends, and apply what remains of the idea (a considerable remnant) to God. Strictly speaking, the terms *was* and *will be* have nothing to do with God. He *is,* simply.

Take this same basic notion of limitlessness and apply it now not to time but to all good or positive attributes or characteristics or qualities, and we arrive at the idea of infinity or absolute *perfection.* The good, the true, and the beautiful need neither description nor recommendation for the normal human being, because our instant, constant relish for these splendors is built in, and is not susceptible to final discouragement. Is God good, and therefore loving and lovable? Infinitely so. Is God true, and therefore faithful and fair and swift to help? Infinitely so. Is God the perfection of beauty, the supreme loveliness, the unmarred, indefectible satisfaction of all the noblest yearnings of the human heart? Infinitely so. *Deus perpulcher,* wrote an ancient writer with a kind of loving rapture: "God so beautiful."

It is always embarrassing, and not a little ridiculous, to undertake to describe God. But God will smile at our pathetic struggle to capture Him in words. He is infinitely decent about such matters.

If God is, and if God is even approximately thus and so, what shall we say, in addition to that personal quality already noted, about the fundamental relationship between God and man?

What God is to man, factually and before all else, is man's Maker. The most basic relationship between God and man is the relationship between creator and creature.

It must be understood that the creative act of God which terminates in a now existing creature is not an event of the past. What keeps every existent object in being is God's sustaining will, the continuation of His creative act. If God, for an instant, were to cease willing my existence, I would not simply die. I would be annihilated; I would altogether vanish. I would lapse into nothingness; there would be no I. What the rational creature must grasp, therefore, and must grasp with clarity and finality, is his essential position vis-à-vis almighty God. Man is *dependent* upon God.

2
The Acts of Religion

Comparative religion is a fascinating study which need not at all be, as it sometimes is, misleading. It is no end astonishing, not to say staggering, what men have done and unquestionably will do for the god or gods in whom they believe. As an obscure but laboring contemporary writer has put it, "Now the practical process of worshipping any god and most of all the true God has always posed a slight problem for human beings: just how do you worship a god? Guided by a sure and deep instinct, people have realized that there must be something more to religion (for that is what the worship of God is) than the periodic mouthing of formulae; they saw clearly that a man ought to *do* something for his god, even if that meant, as it sometimes did, *not* doing something in honor of the god. So men prostrated their bodies before idols, they sang and danced and, in the jollier religions, got drunk; they taxed their physical endurance in all sorts of ways, they fasted and sat immobile for hours and scourged themselves and sprinkled ashes on their heads" (McCorry: *More Blessed Than Kings*). It might be added that men zealously honored their god by even stranger procedures, as by broiling infants and strangling young boys and violating virgins and drawing and quartering men of a different religious view.

7

Nevertheless, the question is valid, and remains. What can a man do for God (let us confine our discussion to the veritable Deity), and therefore what ought a man to do for God, seeing that this man does truly believe in God?

There are three possibilities and, therefore, three duties. These procedures are obviously not alternative, but complementary. Taken together, they constitute the practice of true religion.

First, man can do for God that which man would do for any other real person with whom he stood in any kind of cordial relationship: he can talk to God. That is, man can pray. Since he can, he should.

It comes wide of our present intent to enter into anything like a discussion of prayer. We beg leave, therefore, to confine ourselves to a single observation on a large and urgent matter. Prayer is neither a luxury nor an emergency procedure nor a fad nor an experience nor an escape. It is a plain duty. The first requirement of prayer is that, like any genuine duty, it be performed. All other questions can come later. A cleric of sorts recently broke into newspaper print to warn parents not to make children say prayers which they do not understand. We trust that the same naïve parents will employ the identical procedure in matters like cleanliness and manners. Don't make small fry take baths until they fully grasp the meaning of the bath. Do not teach them manners whose bent and inner significance the little savages do not comprehend. If we must be mad, let us at least, like normal psychopaths, be consistent in our madness.

Surely it is truthful to say that there has never been a religion without precepts or prohibitions of some kind. The twin notion of *hoc faciendum, hoc vitandum,* "this must be done, this avoided," is to be found in every religious system that has ever appeared on the face of the earth. Now precepts demand obedience. Obedience to behavioral precepts constitutes morality. What man can and must do for God in addition to praying to Him is to obey Him, to lead a moral life, to be simply and solidly a good man.

There arises, then, the significant question: Is there anything else believing man can do for God? Is there any other element in the practice of religion besides prayer and morality? We search for the answer in three deep mines of truth: in man's nature, in his history, in the religious revelation God has made to man. In each case the answer is affirmative, and always the same.

Literally nothing is more instinctive to man than gift giving. Man is not an angel. He is so heartily material that what he experiences in his invisible, impalpable, but undeniable soul tends at once to spill over into bodily reactions, movements, and signs. He is worried; he finds that he cannot eat. He is heartbroken; the salty tears flow down his cheeks. He is overjoyed; he must tell someone. Man entertains some kind of regard or high opinion or affection or fear or calculation with regard to another; he gives that other a gift.

The person who receives the gift may have no need of it; indeed it might be argued that the majority of gifts are spectacularly useless. No matter. "O reason not the need!" cries poor old tormented Lear. A gift bears no essential relation to need. If it answers a need, well and good. If not, well and good. Gift giving flows from subtler impulses than that which leads us to give a quarter to a shabby tramp.

A gift is manifestly a sign or a symbol. It gives visible, material expression to an interior attitude. Essentially, such interior attitudes may easily be catalogued. I offer a present to a highly placed person in token of my recognition of his superior and my inferior position. In short, I make a gift in order to honor that personage. I bring a present in gratitude. This gift is now a return gift, whereby I acknowledge a debt and try, symbolically at least, to pay off my debt. Again, I offer a present as an apology; the offered object says to the recipient for me: "I am sorry for my neglect, my ill behavior, for the pain or inconvenience I brought upon you." Lastly, I may make a gift with careful reckoning — in the hope of getting something in return. This procedure is known technically as the Political Ploy.

It should be noted that a certain vague but profound idea accompanies and colors all these reasons for giving a present. That is the notion that by the giving and accepting of the gift, the two parties are at once brought into closer and more amiable relationship. The point is significant.

Anyone is welcome to devise further motives for gift making, but they will be found to be strictly reducible to the promptings here enumerated.

Certain other aspects of the gift are too obvious to delay us. That which is given must certainly belong to the giver, else he has no right to give it. That which is given must be truly given, not merely loaned or shown; there is a real transfer of ownership. That which is given, in proportion to its value (either absolutely or with reference to the giver) and in proportion to its closeness of connection with the giver, will become that much more valuable and significant as a gift.

As man has always and deeply experienced the impulse to make a gift to another man, so man has invariably and more deeply experienced the impulse to make a gift to God. Historically, men have almost always and almost everywhere made such gifts. As far as supernatural revelation is concerned, almighty God has unmistakably signified that He desires and welcomes such gifts — obviously not for what they are, but for what they mean.

The religious and proper name for the giving of a present to God is, of course, *sacrifice.*

Says the *Catholic Encyclopedia:* "Sacrifice is the offering of a sense-perceptible gift to the Deity as an outward manifestation of our veneration for Him and with the object of attaining communion with Him."

At once the following keen observation is added: "Strictly speaking, however, this offering does not become a sacrifice until a real change has been effected in the visible gift — by slaying it, shedding its blood, burning it or pouring it out." This capital point must receive further attention.

3

The Pattern of Sacrifice

In point of sheer historical fact, to what degree is the ritual act of sacrifice found in the many and varied religions with which this fumbling, bumbling world of men has experimented in the course of time? Once more we beg leave to lean upon the learning of the *Catholic Encyclopedia:* "Pure Buddhism, Mohammedanism and Protestantism . . . have no real sacrifice; apart from these there is and has been no developed religion which has not accepted sacrifice as an essential portion of its cult." The phenomenon of sacrifice in religion is, therefore, the rule rather than the exception. Moreover, amid the considerable variations that adorned and sometimes disfigured the religious act of sacrifice, a certain basic standardization or common denominator is readily observable.

The necessary first step in sacrifice is the preliturgical one, and therefore it must be regarded simply as the required preparation. The material object which will be offered must be selected. Suffice it to say that practically everything under the sun has at one time or another been offered by men to their deities. Horses, steers, oxen, goats, sheep, pigs, birds; cakes of rice and barley, toasted ears of corn, flour, bread, salt, wine, and oil; wool, flax, incense; fish (by the Babylonians, never among the Jews) — all these and more made material for religious sacrifice.

Clearly, though, there was everywhere a steady preference for the living as against the inanimate or even vegetable thing. The fact must be pondered.

To begin with, in any primitive or simple society the animal, and especially the domestic animal, was valuable. It is interesting, for example, that Jewish law forbade the use of wild animals in sacrifice. The bull, the cow, the heifer, the goat, the lamb — these are possessions which nomadic or agricultural people come by hardly, mind most carefully, and part with reluctantly. The heartrending parable of the prophet Nathan to King David aroused the wrath of that unsuspecting monarch, as well it might. So, when a farmer possessed but a single lamb, and then brought that as a sacrifice to the Lord, that poor fellow was making a sacrifice, indeed.

Moreover, there is always a closer bond between the man and the domestic animal than between the man and anything else except another human being. Everyone knows how even the most unsentimental and unsusceptible person can become attached to a pet. It is said that St. John the Evangelist kept a pet bird, that Cardinal Richelieu (a different type) loved his cat, that St. Jerome was generally accompanied by a young lion (a legend which led Chesterton to observe that it was a good way to keep from being lionized). Modern people spend millions of dollars annually on animals, and we all know about the lunatics who would halt medical research with animals even if it meant that many future babies would die for want of such research.

But there is more to the connection between men and animals than value and affection. A man and his dog or cat or horse share a priceless, irreplaceable thing, an ultimately indescribable thing: life. What a human being dreads above all else is the ending of his life. The same terrible event, when it happens to a beast, fills the human being with horror and sadness and pain. Death is so frightfully definitive. When a man looks upon the still body of the warm-blooded, vital animal that lately had romped with such relish, he is stricken not only by grief for a lost friend, but with nameless terror at the searing sight of what he himself one day must be: dead.

The reason why blood, as we shall see, plays so prominent a part in religious sacrifice is not far to seek. The blood means the life. The blood, once spilled, is forever spilled.

The gift or, to use the proper term in the only kind of sacrifice that concerns us, the *victim* has now been selected. By and large, what was then the standard procedure in the ritual act of religious sacrifice?

First, there was the bringing forward, the ritual *offering* of the victim. At once the idea of a solemn or festive procession suggests itself, and that is exactly what commonly took place. The animal had been meticulously groomed; it had probably been hung with sweet-smelling garlands and bright draperies; its horns, if any, may have been polished or gilded or painted. Now the lowing or bleating beast is led forward to the shouts and hymns and prayers of the accompanying worshipers. The priest — for sacrifice always implies a priest — in splendid raiment and wearing the special badges of his high state, receives the victim with prayers and lustrations and blessings. The priest, God's man and the people's, is offering to God his own and the people's gift.

Next came the central act, the immolation, the slaying, the destruction of the victim.

It is by no means unthinkable that a thoughtful religious man of our day might experience a genuine repugnance for this central act in ancient sacrifice. For one thing, since he is much more sentimental about animals than were his fathers, his sympathies tend to be with the sacrificial victim rather than with the relatively carefree worshipers. He may even, on the subject of vicarious guilt, be polite but dubious. Above all, the butchering of a perfectly good animal seems such a wicked waste, does it not?

That word *butchering* is worth a moment's notice. Never, in all the most abundant sacrifices of the past, were so many animals butchered in religious faith as are daily butchered in our culture for our tables. We perverse mortals, badly damaged by original sin, find it so difficult to avoid the assumption that what is given to us for our pleasure or our palates is put to excellent use, but what is given to God is wasted. Besides, a fair-minded religious man will seriously ask himself just how the ownership of any object can be certainly and exclusively turned over to God without destroying that object. Take it as a fact of the most natural kind that if, in sacrifice, the object offered to God were not destroyed, there would not for long be a sacrifice. It would very soon be a shenanigan. Someone would get the gift, but it wouldn't be God.

The sacrificial immolation was a ritual procedure, of course. The throat of the victim was slashed in a particular way, and the blood was carefully received in sacred vessels.

Here we must pause to observe carefully what has been mentioned previously and what may be now expressed in the words of an authority: "Everywhere from China to Ireland the *blood* is the chief thing, the center of the sacrifice; in the blood lies the power." Why is this? "But the propitiation for the guilt-laden soul is accomplished by the blood in virtue of the life contained in it, which (life) belongs to the Lord of life and death" (Bähr, quoted in the *Catholic Encyclopedia* article). Life, the supreme thing, belongs to the Supreme Being. It is His gift. When the gift is given back to Him in expiation, the supreme satisfaction for sin has been made. And again we repeat: the blood is the life.

We read in the ninth chapter of the Epistle to the Hebrews: *When he had finished reading the provisions of the law to the assembled people, Moses took blood, the blood of calves and goats, took water, and scarlet-dyed wool, and hyssop, sprinkled the book itself, and all the people, and said, This is the blood of the covenant which God has prescribed to you. The tabernacle, too, and all the requisites of worship he sprinkled in the same way with blood; and the law enjoins that blood shall be used in almost every act of purification; unless blood is shed, there can be no remission of sins.*

The *Catholic Encyclopedia* explains: "The blood obtained by the slaying exerts its expiatory power first on the altar, where the soul of the victim symbolically laden with sin comes into contact with the purifying and sanctifying power of God."

The slaying ceremony ended with the burning, in whole or in part, of the quartered body of the victim.

One would suppose that the act of sacrifice was now concluded. In fact, another and most significant ceremony frequently followed. This was the sacred banquet.

Man, who is in part animal, must eat like any animal. This is manifestly a matter in which man has no option. Like it or not — he generally does — man must eat, and if, for some odd reason, he will not or cannot eat, then food or its equivalent must be gotten into him somehow. Now it is a curious fact that although we commonly perform all other strictly corporal and especially animal functions in private, we tend to eat in company, and this despite the evident truth that eating is not the prettiest or tidiest process in the world. One senses here a small hint, provided by the instinctive behavior of the human animal, that there is more to the act of eating than appears. Indeed, there is the same suggestion about eating as there is about blood. Both mean life. In a word, the necessary, brute act of eating does not lack a certain mysticism.

At this point the professional historian, the anthropologist, and the student of comparative religion all step forward as an amiable troika in order to point out to us that the act of communal eating has always figured largely in religious cere-monial, and chiefly in connection with the act of sacrifice.

It might not be possible to sort out all the secret impulses (divine revelation aside) that led men to associate eating with sacrifice. There would be, surely, the ever present com-munal instinct to eat at the same table and partake of the same food. There would be profound seeking for new strength, and new strength is sensed in the act of eating. There would be the natural desire for personal gratification even in religious activity, and the readiest way to come by personal pleasure is by eating and drinking. There would be, we must suppose, a kind of commonplace feeling which would be strong in people for whom fresh meat was an extreme luxury: since the luscious flesh is here and ready and since the god has no immediate use for it, why not eat it?

But all this overlooks the deep-down mysticism of religious eating. What every religion promises and what every religious man comes seeking is divine union: purifying and sanctifying contact and more than contact with the god — or goddess. In the temple of Aphrodite Pandemos overlooking old Corinth some thousand temple prostitutes did duty for Aphrodite, thereby providing alleged divine union, in grossest form, for all comers who could afford a donation to the temple.

Still, the more convenient and more fastidious and more usual mode of divine union, and one more directly connected with sacrifice, was the sacred eating. The victim had been given over to the god, and was now the property of the god; hence it was itself now holy. The god symbolically partakes of the sacred flesh. The worshiper eats; and thus not only do he and the god sup together — itself a mystical sharing — but the worshiper eats of that which is now somehow but really an extension of the god himself. The divine union is achieved. The god is honored and pleased. The worshiper is replete and sanctified. There is peace, there is joy. Presumably there is holiness.

It must be evident that religious sacrifice, like all very ambitious and exalted human undertakings, lends itself to debasing and diabolical caricature. The man of religion cannot afford to forget that he must take the world of the supernatural as it is, and not as he might wish it. If a man seeks God, he must expect to find the fallen enemy of God (*Satan* means "adversary") blocking his path. If a man would traffic with an angel named Michael, he may anticipate dealings with an angel named Lucifer. If there really is a Christ, there really will be an Antichrist. Where there is the Mass, there may yet be the Black Mass.

In addition to the unlovely goings-on at Corinth one could easily list other revolting variations on the sacrificial theme. The ancient Greeks drank deep and coupled freely at the spring festival in honor of Dionysus, god of the vine. The Romans piously honored Persian Mithra by the grisly *taurobolium:* "the worshipers . . . let the warm blood of a just-slaughtered steer flow over their naked bodies as they lay in a trench." The Phoenicians, who posed a constant threat of idolatrous infection to Israel, offered to Baal and Astarte the sacrifice of a maiden's chastity. And, of course, there has appeared so often in history and in so many places on this green earth that which becomes so horribly logical on all the premises of liturgical religion: human sacrifice. We will never know how many babies were devoured by brazen-faced Moloch. In the shocking murals of Mexican Diego Rivera one can still see the lofty sanctuary steps of the pagan temples running with human blood. In South America today we find in a cave the pathetic skeleton of the nine-year-old boy who had been slowly strangled in his rich, ceremonial robes. Satan, the beast, is the ape of God.

Let us leave all this horror and return to the holy thing. What shall be said of the specific reasons or motives for religious sacrifice?

What shall be said is that those motives are few; they are always the same; and they are exactly the motives for all gift giving. The first purpose of religious sacrifice is simply to honor God by recognizing His majesty and sovereignty. The second motive is to thank Him. The third is to make atonement for sin against Him. The last is to implore Him for help in our needs.

For these reasons Moses and Melchisedech offered sacrifice. For these reasons Abraham would have slain his son Isaac. For these reasons the Jewish high priest entered the Holy of Holies. For these reasons Christ died on Calvary. For these reasons the Catholic priest says Mass.

4

The Christ-Sacrifice

The event in history which is *the* event in history, since all else either led up to it or slopes away from it, is what Christian theology calls the Incarnation. God did once become man.

Says Dr. Karl Adam: "The belief that the Godhead could manifest itself in human form is not infrequently a constituent of pagan mythologies. But in all these pagan incarnations the purely human loses its individual significance, its individual value. It becomes an empty husk, a phantom of the divine. Docetism (the notion that Christ *seemed* to be, but was not actually man) runs in the blood of all those mythologies. Of quite another kind is the Christian mystery of the Incarnation. The humanity of Christ is here not an illusion; its purpose is not merely to make the divine visible; it is not simply the perceptible form in which the Godhead presents itself to us, the perceptible point at which the divine flames forth. On the contrary, the humanity of Christ has its own distinctive form, its own distinctive function. It is precisely in virtue of its human quality that it is the way, the means, the sacrament by which God draws near to us and redeems us. In the whole range of religious history we can find no analogue to this fundamental Christian doctrine of the redemptive significance of Christ's humanity" (Karl Adam: *The Son of God*).

So then, the Second Person of the blessed and adorable Trinity became man, became truly man; but not simply (appealing as is this aspect of the truth) in order to become one of us. God became man for a purpose, and this purpose shows itself as a positive preoccupation — we almost said *obsession* — with Christ as He is portrayed in the four Gospels.

From first utterance to all but last, as our Savior speaks in the Gospels, His view is single and simple, His path is clear, His mind is undivided. When He is only twelve and by His abrupt absence has lacerated His Mother's tender heart, He seems surprised that there can be any doubt or question about His first task and duty: *Could you not tell that I must needs be in the place which belongs to My Father?* At death's door He says from the cross: *It is achieved.* In His first recorded word Christ said He had a work to do. In His penultimate word He says He has done it.

The work was that of redemption. The question is, what was the mode, the method, the manner of redemption? Christ came to redeem us. But *how* did He redeem us?

A Christian child would say: Christ redeemed us by His death on Calvary. True. But it is of highest consequence that that death on Calvary be not misunderstood and thus, however oddly, be underestimated.

There are two ways of looking at the death of Christ, even in its redemptive light.

In the first view, Christ, whoever or whatever He was beyond what appeared, was clearly a most lofty personality and leader of the type that blesses this poor old earth on the rarest occasions. Just as clearly, He was a properly accredited messenger or agent from almighty God. Now this Christ preached a message of exquisite beauty and astonishing power, and, in conjunction with the message, He founded a definite movement which manifestly was not to end with Him. As so often happens in a world which is largely either blind or evil, this exalted Leader outraged the established powers and, after a brief struggle, was destroyed by them. But magnificent as He had been in life, He was yet more magnificent in adversity, suffering, and death. Having warned His faithful followers that they must expect to fare little better than He, He died heroically. His burning words, His prodigious example, above all the majestic manner of His death — these deathless forces, like unquenchable beacons, will always light men the way to eternal life. In short, Christ redeemed men by dying an exemplary martyr for all.

Such a view of the life and death of Christ is not Catholic. It may be questioned whether it is Christian. Let us attend to the judgment of non-Catholic Albert Schweitzer: "The Jesus of Nazareth who . . . proclaimed the moral code of the Kingdom of God, founded the kingdom of heaven on earth, and died in order to consecrate his life, has never existed. It is a figure projected by Rationalism, made animate by Liberalism, and clothed in an historical garment by modern theology."

The other view of the redemptive death of Christ may be summarized by the use of two key words. Christ was not simply a teacher and a leader and a hero and a martyr and an undying inspiration. He was a *priest,* and His death was a *sacrifice.*

It may have been accidental that the death of Christ coincided with the Jewish Passover, when was celebrated again by God's people the ancient, salvific sacrifice of the paschal lamb. It may have been mere, if moving, metaphor when John the Baptist, at the very outset, pointed to Christ and said: *Look, this is the Lamb of God: look, this is He who takes away the sin of the world.* It may be only splendidly literary that the Epistle to the Hebrews celebrates the priesthood of Christ and His supreme act of sacrifice in and by His own blood. It may be bias to detect a singular, ambivalent tone, proper both to a priest and to a victim, in such Christ sayings as: *There is a baptism I must needs be baptized with, and how impatient I am for its accomplishment!* and, at the beginning of the Last Supper: *I have longed and longed to share this paschal meal with you before My passion.* Yes, all this may be accident or incident or metaphor or allegory or bias or whatever. But it is not. These are all small signs pointing, like the devoted Baptist, to one truth about one Person, the big truth about a divine Person: Christ was a priest, and His death was a sacrifice.

Let us recall and verify the first two acts in liturgical sacrifice. The victim Christ was led from the virginal womb of His Mother by His heavenly Father, by the Holy Spirit, and by Christ the priest through all the highways and byways of His mortal life, through the lanes of cheering, all unwitting people of Palm Sunday, to the rocky altar of Calvary. And on that altar hill Christ the victim was immolated by Christ the priest. Indeed, the poor victim was fiercely hacked and slain by impious hands, but the hands were but hands, red and guilty with blood as they were, and the wits were all but witless. The Savior Himself said it: *They do not know what it is they are doing.*

But what of the third act in religious sacrifice, what about the sacred eating?

As every Christian knows well, something else, something

of incalculable significance and importance, intervened between the lifelong offering and the final immolation of Christ the victim. It was what Christians will always call, with boundless love and endless meaning, the Last Supper.

Then He took bread, and blessed and broke it, and gave it to them, saying: This is My body, given for you; do this for a commemoration of Me. And so with the cup, when supper was ended: This cup, He said, is the new testament, in My blood which is to be shed for you.

Catholic theology has always insisted on three major truths that lie hidden in these sublime, these heavenly words. First, there is the truth called *transubstantiation:* that, in some manner which lies totally beyond the reach of human comprehension, that bread and that wine did actually become the body and blood of Christ Jesus. Second, there is the truth, almost equally beyond human wisdom to explain, that this singular and evidently momentous action of Christ in the supper room is mystically connected with, continuous with, and somehow identical with the death of Christ that would soon follow on Calvary. Third, there is the stupendous, staggering truth contained in the solemn Christ mandate: *Do this for a commemoration of Me.*

These three truths make one truth: here is instituted, to the glory of God and for the salvation of men, the holy sacrifice of the Mass.

We adore Thee, O Christ, and we bless Thee. . . .

5

The Christian Sacrifice

It must be evident to the Catholic people whom the Canon of the Mass, speaking directly to God, terms *plebs Tua sancta, Your holy people,* that all those who undertake to speak or write about the Holy Sacrifice will say, essentially, the same things. When, moreover, a Catholic spokesman of towering stature has summarized in almost ideal fashion the fixed and unchanging truths about the Mass, the lesser commentators will be wise to tread gratefully in such giant footsteps. Thus, gratefully, we rehearse here in humbler words the admirable exposition of the Mass in *Meditations Before Mass* by the celebrated European theologian, Monsignor Romano Guardini.

There are five aspects to the Mass. It is an institution, a memorial, a covenant, a reality, and a banquet.

The service of prayer which the believer renders to the divine Majesty may be performed in one of two ways: on personal initiative or by direction. When a Catholic, kneeling before our Lord at, say, Benediction, murmurs: "Lord Christ, I need You," he is praying on personal initiative. When he joins in the singing of the *Tantum Ergo* he is praying by direction. In the first case the individual, guided by what some would call *impulse* and others *grace,* speaks to God when and where he chooses and in the words of his choice. In the second case the individual speaks to God in a strange tongue with the words of a useful fellow named Thomas

Aquinas at the instance and even insistence of the Church. The Church has competently determined that if you are going to have Benediction of the Blessed Sacrament you are going to sing or say the *Tantum Ergo*. Certain energetic natures may not care much for this directed mode of prayer, but most of us, understandably somewhat tongue-tied in the presence of *tantum . . . sacramentum,* are grateful for whatever prompting we can get from Aquinas and the Bride of Christ.

Now the Mass emphatically belongs in this second category of religious activity. It is not an impulse; it is an institution. Says Guardini: "The Mass . . . does not arise each time from the individual's or the congregation's relation to God, but descends from God to the believer, demanding that he acknowledge it, entrust himself to it, *do* it." We suggest that these words merit pondering. They provide the adequate answer to those who wonder why the Catholic Church steadfastly requires people to do what they do not always perfectly comprehend. The truth here touched upon is a large one. In not a few moments of human life it is advisable first to do something, and afterward to begin to wonder how and why.

This institution, the Mass, comes directly from Christ and is entrusted by Christ to His Church. It follows that the Church may, and will, modify the liturgy of the Mass. It follows that no one else will dare tamper in any way with the prescribed ceremonial of the Mass. Both priest and people must ever remember that private impulse has no place in a sacred institution.

Nothing is clearer, from the very nature and even the words of the Mass, than its memorial quality. *Do this,* said Christ our Lord at the moment of institution, *for a commemoration of Me.* No one will dispute that the fallible, forgetful human being needs regularly to be reminded of all sorts of truths and obligations, including, sad to say, matters of such painful tenderness that we are ashamed when we find we have forgotten them. The writer recently had occasion to visit the grave of his mother and father. He had difficulty finding it.

Of what are we reminded in and by and throughout the Mass? Not, as in other memorial services, of a life process or a universal truth or a doctrine or a cosmic or national event or a myth. The Mass is a memorial of a Person. When the priest genuflects immediately after the Consecration of the Mass he whispers, in the exalted Personality which is then his: *Haec quotiescumque feceritis, in Mei memoriam facietis.* The priest is closely quoting Paul, who is quoting Luke, who is quoting Christ. The words mean: *As often as you shall do this, in memory of Me will you do it.*

More yet. The Mass is a perpetual reminder not only of a Person and *that* Person, but likewise of His destiny; that is, of His redemptive death. Again Paul: *So it is the Lord's death that you are heralding, whenever you eat this bread and drink this cup, until He comes.* In consequence, every Mass, since it is a sacrifice, is not only a reminder of our essential relationship as creatures to God our Creator, but also a reminder of our relationship as redeemed to Christ our Redeemer. *A great price was paid to ransom you,* says St. Paul in awe. We may say, then, that every Mass is a reminder of the destinies of both Christ and the Christian.

There is a word which all four recorders (Matthew, Mark, Luke, Paul) use in setting down the institution of the Eucharist. That word is the Latin *testamentum,* which is a translation of the Greek *diatheke.* Strictly, the term means a last will or disposal of earthly property, but the scholars assure us that in almost all the thirty-three cases where the word occurs in the New Testament it means *covenant* rather than *last will*. The Eucharist was indeed our Savior's testament or last will; but much more, it was the new covenant or solemn pact between God and man. Almighty God had entered into a binding covenant with the Jewish people, and that contract, as the Epistle to the Hebrews explicitly tells us, had been ratified and sanctified in the blood of animal sacrifices. The effect of the pact is described in the Old Testament: *I will be your God, and you will be My people.* The people of Israel were bound by this covenant, as the prophets kept telling them. But so was God; bound by His abounding love.

Now the Lord Christ, God's Son, celebrates for the last time the paschal supper which renewed the ancient pact between God and Israel. Then, in His own body and blood and in anticipation of and continuity with the sacrificial destruction of the morrow, Christ establishes the new covenant, the new pact, the new agreement, the new contract between holy God and sinful man. *Et antiquum documentum novo cedat ritui: The old covenant gives way to the new.* Again God and believing man are bound to one another, but now, because of such a new Priest and Mediator, they are bound together in a love that can be contained in no description. Now more surely than ever will God be faithful to His pledged word. Now, beyond question, if man will do but a little, little he, animal that he is, will look upon the face of God forever.

Perhaps the most difficult aspect of the Mass to expound is, oddly, its reality. The reason for the difficulty is simple: there is no word with which we can define the reality of the Mass. The point is that we are faced here with a theological truth that can only be expressed in something like an algebraic formula. When, in algebra, we say that $x = y$, we are trying to express a matter of considerable subtlety. We do not exactly mean that x is absolutely identical with y, because in that event there would be no x, only two y's. Yet we mean that x is in the strictest way equivalent to y, so that they are inter-changeable and x can always stand for y. Perhaps the only way to phrase the situation is to say that $x = y$ means that x is exactly y, only not exactly.

There *is* a difference between Calvary and the Mass. On Calvary Christ was physically slain, His blood was visibly shed. In the Mass Christ does not physically die again, His blood is now mystically shed. When that has been said, we must immediately add: Calvary *is* the Mass, and the Mass *is* Calvary. The difference does not make any difference.

Finally, the Mass is a sacred eating. *We have a cup that we bless,* writes St. Paul; *is not this cup we bless a participation in Christ's blood?* Bread is for eating, and bread is broken in preparation for that eating. A cup is for drinking. Of course. *You eat this bread and drink this cup,* says Paul again, all obedient to our Savior's imperative: *Take, eat . . . Drink, all of you, of this.*

In the Christian Sacrifice, as in all those ancient, feeble sacrifices that were but poor candles to the sun, the last act in the holy ritual is the sacred banquet.

When he (Judas) *had gone out* — and when, at this point, God's beloved and divine Son, our Redeemer and Priest, had instituted the Holy Eucharist, the first Mass had been said, and the first Holy Communion received — *Jesus said, Now the Son of Man has achieved His glory, and in His glory God is exalted.*

Reverently we might add: and in that *glory* pitiful and imperiled man is at last safe and secure and holy and at peace.

6

The Catholic and the Mass

Would it be possible to summarize, with a view to weekly and perhaps daily practice, the habitual knowledge which will inform and thus form the Catholic mind in relation to the Mass? Let us make the attempt.

Above all else, the Catholic must be clear on the essential point of what the Mass *is*. The Mass is a prayer, but it is more than a prayer. The Mass is a religious service, but not simply another religious service. The Mass is worship of God, but a most particular form of worship of God. The Mass is the highest of all religious acts, the act of sacrifice; and it is actually and in deed the perfect religious sacrifice, the sacrifice of Calvary resumed and repeated and re-enacted.

The attentive participant in the Mass will be sharply aware of the three parts of the Mass which correspond to the three successive acts in religious sacrifice. These parts are the Offertory, the Canon, and the Communion.

Almost as urgent is a definitive understanding of who it is that offers the Mass. The Mass is a single, indivisible act, yet it is offered by a kind of trinity of persons. The first offerer of the Sacrifice is, of course, the One who did offer the sacrifice of redemption, Christ the High Priest. The second offerer is the visible representative, vicar and agent of the Redeemer, that other Christ, the priest. Here, incidentally, we touch lightly but firmly on the deepest meaning of the Catholic priest. The priest means the Mass. No priest, no Mass.

What the layman must see as clearly is that the third offerer of the Sacrifice is *himself* as a living, present member of the assembled community of the faithful. With Christ and Christ's priest, Christ's people offer Christ in sacrifice to Christ's Father. The Holy Spirit should be asked to make this realization exceedingly real and vivid and powerful in the lay mind.

Next, we will regularly advert to the familiar truth which we learned in our catechism as "the ends of the Mass," the reasons or objectives for which the Sacrifice is offered. They are, as we have observed, the universal motives for all religious sacrifice: adoration, or the recognition and proclamation of the majesty of God and our total dependence upon Him; thanksgiving; expiation, reparation, atonement; and supplication. For this cause alone the Mass would be the perfect prayer, for it is all prayer.

As for the efficacy of the Mass, the Catholic will be completely convinced that the Mass, to put the matter with the utmost mildness, does him good. He may reflect that the absolute value of the Mass is always infinite, because of the infinite, august Person who primarily offers it and is offered in it. Perhaps more realistically the Catholic with any sense of either history or the supernatural will know quite firmly that the Mass means the faith. Where the Mass is, the faith is. Where the Mass flourishes, the faith flourishes. Where the Mass disappears, the faith in time will disappear. One discerns in this profound truth the adequate explanation of the evident fact that certain allegedly Catholic countries are more Catholic in appearance and in theory than in fact. Here too lies the secret reason for a strong correlation. Where the Mass is loved, religious vocations abound. Where vocations abound, the Mass is not only multiplied, but more generally loved.

It is now widely grasped that the ideal in Mass attendance is not attendance. It is participation. The faithful who are present at Mass will associate and identify themselves as intimately as may be with the priest at the altar and thus with Christ on the altar. Hence the layman at Mass will ideally say the prayers which the priest is saying, observe, to the best of his ability and comprehension, the actions which the priest ritually performs, and join in the liturgical dialogue of the sacrificial action. This participation will not always be easy of practice. However, what counts is interior will and desire and comprehension rather than external precision. Happily, though, even the external precision of participation is steadily improving in our day.

Lastly, the layman will be aware of, indeed he will have experienced, the particular effects or benefits of the Mass. The Mass purifies; the Mass strengthens; the Mass brings peace. In the simpler formula, the Mass increases supernatural charity, and, of course, charity means love. But let no one of us who believe in Christ and His sacrifice forget for a moment that the Mass, a corporate and communal act, ought of its nature to deepen not only a man's love for God, but — what is frequently far more difficult — a man's authentic, unsentimental, and operative love for his fellowman. The liturgy of the Church calls the Eucharist *vinculum unitatis et pacis: the bond of unity and peace.*

7

The Ordinary of the Mass

The short essays that here follow are an effort, however imperfect, to aid the Catholic layman to come to a better knowledge of and love for and participation in the Mass. The undertaking has been to explain, as unpretentiously as may be, the liturgical prayers of what is called the Ordinary of the Mass, that considerable portion of the ritual which changes little or not at all from day to day.

The writer hesitates, with the caution of middle years, to proclaim that he has truly learned this or that in the course of his life. Nevertheless, he begins to sense what was told him long ago by a wiser man. It is the truth that can only be expressed thus simply: the Mass is everything.

I. THE FOREMASS

1. *I will go to the altar of God, to God who gives joy to my youth* (the opening words of every Mass).

The highest of all religious acts, the action which is most pleasing to God and most profitable for men, is the act of sacrifice. The most sublime of all religious sacrifices, the completely perfect one which every other merely prefigured and foreshadowed, is that sacrifice of the cross which was once achieved on Calvary and which is yet mystically renewed in every Mass. No intelligent Catholic need be told that the Mass is the functional or operative center of his life, for, in truth, the Mass is the accurate measure of the Catholic. Those who are uncomprehending or bored or grudging or absent at Mass are uncomprehending or bored or grudging or essentially absent Catholics.

As has been said again and again, the ideal in assistance at Mass goes considerably beyond physical presence. What is wanted is enlightened participation in the communal act of sacrifice. (It is painful, but only honest, to remark that priests who celebrate Mass at breakneck speed, thus precluding intelligent participation, are the leaders and champions of liturgical incomprehension.) The evident first requirement for rational sharing in anything is some fairly clear understanding of what is being said and what is being done.

Every Mass begins as every Catholic action should begin: *In the name of the Father and of the Son and of the Holy Spirit.* The priest then makes a simple declaration of intent: *I will go to the altar of God.* The response of the people — stated no less than three times in this initial dialogue — is interesting: *To God who gives joy to my youth.* The word *altar* is not repeated, for the altar is but a symbol; it is the meeting place of God and man. Priest and people now draw near to God. As they do so, the key words for their action are *joy* and *youth*.

The liturgy of Holy Mother Church stands at the opposite pole to religious emotionalism. No one knows better than the Church that emotion in religion cannot be commanded, and that emotion is not automatically to be trusted even when it occurs. Yet repeatedly, in her liturgy, the Church employs, though always calmly, words of feeling, human terms which point to the interior supernatural mood or attitude that becomes man at a particular moment in his intimate dealings with the most high God. We are always safe when we are guided, whether in belief or outlook or mood or feelings, by Mother Church. Every one of us should begin every Mass with *joy*. It is so good, so very good and wonderful and glorious, that we should again be re-enacting the sacrifice of our redemption.

The *youth* which is here mentioned is blessedly unconnected with chronology. It belongs to the old, old lady, clucking and whispering over her beads in the last pew, as it belongs to the restless small fry up front. St. Paul is forever telling us that the supernatural life which, after baptism, we lead *in Christ Jesus* is entirely *new;* it is a fresh and timeless existence into which we are ever newly born. It is neither the soul of man nor the Church nor Christ that grows old. We are all young again, we are strong and vital and vigorous as, under the protecting arms of Mother Church, the young, radiant Bride of Christ, we come joyfully to the altar of God to renew, timelessly, the precious redemptive death of the youthful Christ.

We really need no bell or chime as we enter gladly upon

the Mass. The ringing and the singing sound clear: *I will go to the altar of God; to God who gives joy to my youth.*

2. *The light of Thy presence, the fulfillment of Thy promise, let these be my escort, bringing me safe to Thy holy mountain, to the tabernacle where Thou dwellest* (Ps. 42:3, the opening Psalm of the Mass).

The learned Father Pius Parsch says: "The introduction of the psalm *Judica* among the prayers at the foot of the altar is shrouded in obscurity." He notes an observation of St. Ambrose that Psalm 42 was used as a postbaptismal hymn at Milan in the fourth century. The newly baptized chanted this song as they moved to participate fully, for the first time, in the Eucharistic sacrifice.

Psalm 42, in conjunction with Psalm 41, makes a great cry of longing. It is a song of Israel in exile. The hymn moves between two distinct and even opposite polarities: it is sad and it is joyful, it is depressed and it is confident, it is far from God but it will come near to God. The complexity or paradox, at first glance so odd, is genuinely apt as we who believe in the Mass prepare to celebrate it.

Everyone remembers the curious behavior of Simon Peter on the occasion of the miraculous catch of fish. *At seeing this, Simon Peter fell down and caught Jesus by the knees: Leave me to myself, Lord, he said; I am a sinner.* We would be suspected of frivolity if we were to imagine our beloved Savior answering Peter somewhat in this fashion: "How can I leave you, clinging to Me as you are?" Our blessed Lord needed to make no such remark, for He understood perfectly. Simon Peter in that homely, eloquent scene is, in sober reality, religious man before God: in his unworthiness he dare not come too near; in his utter need, he dare not shrink away.

Such is the fitting dialectic with which we open the ritual of the Mass.

The man is mad who can draw near to the infinite and infinitely holy God without feeling, like a pain, or more like a terror, the measureless distance between himself and the divine Majesty. Wide is the yawning gap between finite and Infinite, between creature and Creator; but fearful is the chasm between the white, blazing holiness of God and the seamy, scabrous sinfulness of fallen and ever falling man. I, this shallow and silly and sinful man, step into God's bright presence out of my dim world of doubtful struggle against evil propensities. Is it any wonder that I cry as if in anguish: *Thou, O God, art all my strength; why hast Thou cast me off? Must I go mourning, with enemies pressing me hard?*

And yet: *I will go up to the altar of God.* How dare I? *The light of Thy presence, the fulfillment of Thy promise, let these be my escort.* . . . On the threshold of the most sublime of all actions, our confidence lies in God's *presence* and God's *promise.*

The nearness of God is not menacing; on the contrary, it is protective and paternal. The answer of God our Lord to our almost despairing cry of unworthiness is exactly the answer of Christ our Lord to abashed Simon Peter: *Do not be afraid.* Let us be convinced that this *is* what the Triune God does say to us at the rightly tremulous beginning of our sacrifice: *Do not be afraid.*

Besides, there stands forever God's *promise.* The blood that will be shed again, all mystically, in this Mass is in truth *the new testament,* the new covenant between God appeased and man redeemed. *This cup, He said, is the new testament, in My blood which is to be shed for you.* A soiled and sinful creature, a guilty son of guilty Adam, might justly stand nervous and unsure as he presents himself to play an actual part in the exalted religious act of sacrifice. Let that man but raise his eyes to the crucifix over the tabernacle. There is the sign — the sign of the cross, the sign of the new and everlasting and redeeming pact between God and man. *Let these be my escort. . . .*

3. *I confess to almighty God . . . that I have very much sinned in thought, word, and deed; through my fault, through my fault, through my most grievous fault* (the *Confiteor,* recited at the foot of the altar at the beginning of every Mass).

Our contemporary culture appears to entertain strong feelings not so much on the matter of guilt as on the subject of guilt feelings. The fact, if it be such, deserves the attention of the thoughtful. Ever since the advent of conscienceless perjury under oath, the abuse of the Fifth Amendment, big-time huckstering, the insanity plea, and quiz programs — in short, ever since the formal disappearance of truth as an ideal in our civilization, it has become not only prohibitively difficult but practically impossible to find anyone, even the most impudent and cynical evildoers, guilty of anything. Having rid ourselves of guilt, it only remains for us to rid ourselves of the annoying hangover, guilt feelings. Progress (to use a word) along these lines is constantly being reported. Juveniles can now steal a car, fornicate, or beat up a passerby with an easy mind and with little fear of retribution.

There would seem to be three alternative possibilities in the matter of guilt feelings. Either a person feels guilt for something he did not do, or he feels guilt for something he certainly did do, or he feels a disproportionate guilt for something which he did do. Let us examine this triple situation.

Everyone agrees that to experience a strong sense of guilt in a connection where one is altogether innocent is a morbidity. Sometimes it does happen that when sorrow befalls or tragedy strikes, the involved and afflicted ones will harshly blame themselves for not having taken some unreal, extreme caution or other, or, even more vaguely, for having displeased Providence in ways unknown. The attitude is neurotic and un-christian, but in most cases it is purely emotional and can be gentled.

Similarly, it is morbid to feel guilt out of all proportion to actual responsibility. Here we encounter the neurosis of scrupulosity, and scrupulosity, beyond doubt, can be a troublesome and even destructive ailment. Still, ought we to suppose that the ailment gives evidence of being any way epidemic in our society? Hardly. There is, on the contrary, a kind of social thinking in our day that would be uproariously comic if it were not so irresponsible. There are more and more nonmarital pregnancies; let us give more sex instruction. Young people do more and more harm with cars; let us be sure they all have cars. More and more people kill; let us modify the penalty for killing. It is small wonder that no one writes satire any longer. Life is too insanely satirical to be satirized.

The final possibility with reference to a sense of guilt is that a rational being feels guilty when he most certainly is guilty. This state or posture is not necessarily compunction or contrition, but it is unquestionably the first step in the direction of compunction or contrition.

Let us Catholics here clarify our thinking once and for

all. Our Holy Mother the Church, together with Christ our Lord, John the Baptist, the apostle Paul, St. Augustine, St. Thomas Aquinas, every reliable Christian authority and every really sane man, is solidly on the side of deep, strong, and abiding guilt feelings as we rational creatures stand before the almighty and most holy God. We *ought* to feel guilty before God, because we *are* guilty.

In Masses for the dead and during Passiontide, Psalm 42 is omitted from the preparatory prayers at the foot of the altar. The *Confiteor,* the open admission of guilt, the cry of sorrow, the beating of the breast, the plea for the intercession of the saints and for the prayers of our fellows — the *Confiteor* is never omitted. It is always said twice: once by the celebrant of the Mass, be he priest or bishop or cardinal or pope; and once by all the people. Standing at the foot of God's altar we do not fret about possible fantasy concerning guilt feelings. We are concerned with reality: with actual guilt and true sorrow and real forgiveness.

4. *May almighty God have mercy upon you, forgive you your sins, and bring you to life everlasting. May the almighty and merciful Lord grant us pardon, absolution, and remission of our sins* (the absolution, after the *Confiteor,* in the prayers at the foot of the altar).

When at the beginning of Mass, the general confession of moral guilt has been made both by celebrant and people, a similarly general absolution is pronounced by the priest. We may first notice about this liturgical moment that the absolution is prayed for, not simply imparted; it is petitionary and intercessory, not judicial and sacramental. This simple prayer does not and cannot supply for the sacrament of penance. Next, we observe that the supplication embraces the entire community. Although the priest first speaks of *you* and *your sins*, he at once, as if on second and better thought, refers to *us* and *our sins*. Third, we can hardly overlook a certain heavy emphasis here as we beg God for *mercy, forgiveness, life everlasting, pardon, absolution, and remission of our sins*.

What is the effect or, at least, the significance of this prayer?

To begin with, neither this urgent petition nor anything else in the Mass directly and efficaciously remits serious sin. (There is, indeed, a most exceptional exception to this veritable principle, but it is of so special a nature that we beg leave to exclude it from the present discussion.) Christ our Lord has left a specific, sacramental instrument for the express purpose of cleansing the soul of grave sin committed after baptism, and the use of this instrument, sacramental confession, is not optional but obligatory if and when mortal sin is committed. Holy Communion does remit venial sin — such remission is one of the secondary effects of the Eucharist — but only on condition of sincere sorrow in the individual for that venial sin. Holy Communion does not wash away the guilt of a grudge or of an intention to seek petty revenge as long as I nurse the grudge or retain the hope and plan for mean retaliation.

If, then, mortal guilt can normally be absolved only in confession and if venial guilt is forgiven, as described, in Holy Communion, what remains as the consequence of this intercessory absolution on the threshold of the Holy Sacrifice?

We suggest that the intent of this prayer is, as in the case of many another liturgical procedure, the awakening in those present and participating of a particular interior disposition:

a disposition of humble, contrite confidence.

Literally throughout the Mass, in one way or another, Holy Mother Church draws attention to the utter holiness of the action that is being performed and the complete unworthiness of those who are performing it. Each day, as His benign Holiness in the Holy City celebrates the Holy Sacrifice, the universal Pastor thrice proclaims, striking his breast: *Lord, I am not worthy.* . . . Mother Church is ever vividly conscious of the monstrosity of self-sufficiency in God's freely adopted sons at any moment, but especially as they enter into the most intimate relationship and even union with God's only-begotten Son in the sacrifice and sacred banquet of the Mass. Every child of Adam without exception needs the interior purification of humble contriteness and sincere sorrow for all evil done, even the slightest and most understandable, as he prepares to perform, with the priest at the altar, the highest act of religion in its ultimate and most perfect form.

Yet the strong, just sense of unworthiness must not be permitted to freeze into the icy paralysis and frigid withdrawal of Jansenism. God does desire that we, even we, offer sacrifice to Him. Christ our Savior does earnestly wish us to be present and concerned and sympathetic (in the fullest sense) as His death is mystically renewed. The Holy Spirit is more than eager to visit and purify us in preparation for that of which we are so unworthy. When the priest at the foot of the altar begs *the almighty and merciful God to grant us pardon, absolution, and remission of our sins,* he means to assure us, in the name of the Holy Mother Church, that God will do just that.

We stand before God's altar all unworthy. The conclusion, however, is not: "Be gone." It is: "Draw near."

5. *We beseech Thee, Lord, by the merits of Thy saints whose relics lie here, and of all the saints, be so good in Thy mercy as to pardon me all my sins* (the first prayer in the Mass as the priest arrives at the altar).

Upon the conclusion of the prefatory prayers of the Mass the priestly celebrant ascends to the altar platform and, quietly reciting the present prayer, kisses the altar table. Both the words and the action are significant.

It is a sublime and most humiliating truth, which every priest ought really to consider deeply, that the celebrant of the Mass acts in three distinct capacities. He becomes, as it were, three exalted personalities as he moves through the Holy Sacrifice. Sometimes the priest-celebrant speaks for the people: *Lord, have mercy; Christ, have mercy; Lord, have mercy.* At the climactic moment of the sacrifice he becomes Christ: *This is My body. . . . This is the chalice of My blood. . . .* At other times the priest is the Church, the Bride of Christ; so it is now, as he first comes to the altar itself.

It must be brought back to the Catholic consciousness that the altar — that is, the altar table, the altar as distinct from the tabernacle, whether the Blessed Sacrament is present in the tabernacle or not — possesses profound liturgical significance. In a way that goes deeper than mere semantics, the altar symbolizes, represents, *is* Christ. This is the reason for all prostration before the altar, as on Good Friday or in the ordination of a priest or consecration of a bishop. When, therefore, the priest reverently kisses the altar, he is performing a glorious function, for he is bestowing upon Christ the Bridegroom the pure nuptial kiss of the Church, His spotless and precious Bride.

Meanwhile the celebrant invokes the intercession of the

saints whose relics lie here (in every Mass altar there must be an altar stone, and in every altar stone repose tiny but authentic fragments of the bones of saints), *and of all the saints.*

The Catholic doctrine which bears the title "the communion of saints" is interwoven in the whole liturgical texture of the Mass. The Catholic, sharply different in this respect from the sincere and devout Protestant, believes firmly in the intercessory power of God's saints, and over and over again in the highest act of his religion he invokes this power and mentions the agents of it. From the *Confiteor,* when, at the very outset, he begs the help of *Blessed Mary ever Virgin, blessed Michael the archangel,* and all the rest, to the Last Gospel, when he reads and hears again that *a man appeared, sent from God, whose name was John,* the Catholic at Mass is steadily conscious of and in contact with God's closest friends and our best benefactors, the saints.

So, at the beginning of the Mass, we are reminded of a lofty, splendid truth which concerns and governs the whole course of the Holy Sacrifice. The Mass is the act of the community; the noble community of the Church; the Church in all her hierarchic order, from Holy Father to latest baptized baby; the Church in that sacred, supercosmic community that embraces the Church militant, the Church suffering, the Church triumphant.

It may be a dark and rainy morning; there may be no one in the church except the priest, a sleepy altar boy, and one old lady; there may be nothing much to see or notice or get excited about. But invisibly the whole earth trembles and the vault of heaven echoes with jubilation as the mighty, holy community that is the Church reaches unfailingly out to God our Lord through Christ His Son and our Victim-Savior.

6. *My eyes are ever toward the Lord; for He shall pluck my feet out of the snare. Look Thou upon me, and have mercy on me, for I am alone and poor. To Thee, Lord, have I lifted up my soul; in Thee, my God, I put my trust; let me not be ashamed* (the Introit of the Mass for the Third Sunday of Lent).

The word *Introit,* a significant liturgical term, comes from a Latin verb meaning *to enter, to go in, to begin.* Of the Introit as it exists in our present Mass the eminent Father Pius Parsch declares flatly that it is "merely rudimentary . . . hardly intelligible. Like a fossil, it is embedded in the Mass, only a reminder now of that once dramatic celebration of the Mass in which the people took such active part."

The only better thing (in the same category) than watching a parade is to be in the parade. Let it not be thought that perceptive people march in a parade in order to be perceived or seen or admired; that motive may be present, but it is secondary. An intelligent and vital man joins a parade in order to play a real part, in order to *participate* in the presumably important and significant event which the parade celebrates.

A ritual ecclesiastical parade is a procession. Holy Mother Church, in her deep wisdom, has always loved processions; in her liturgy she calls for them repeatedly. It is a pity, as well as a mistake, that the contemporary Catholic tends to be shy about walking in a sacred procession. Actually he loves it, as every normal man loves a parade, and the Catholic certainly ought to have some insight into the key truth that a procession is a meaningful thing. Our doubtful friends the Communists are shrewdly crazy about parades. That is why they use them, with music, singing, floats, and all kinds of display, so frequently.

On solemn occasions, which were frequent, the ancient Mass was preceded by a splendid procession from some appointed meeting place to the particular church which had been liturgically selected as the sacred locale for the solemn Sacrifice that day. This church was called the *station;* the station for the third Sunday of Lent, for example, is the Roman church of St. Lawrence Outside-the-Walls. Now the special point is that this procession to the church of the day was not an exclusively clerical affair. Everybody — to employ a modern, highly accurate expression — got into the act.

It is universally recognized that nothing is more natural and more genuinely helpful in the context than that men should sing as they march. For their procession our Christian ancestors naturally sang the songs which our Lord and our Lady and John and Peter and Paul and all the Apostles had sung — the Psalms. A particular psalm was chosen, always with an eye to the station or feast of the day, for the procession of that day. It is the truncated and fossilized remnant of that processional psalm that makes the Introit of our modern Mass.

The attentive Catholic, even while he misses the entrance parade of old, may yet find a double profit in the Introit. The sentiment expressed — joy, compunction, praise, petition, confidence — may be accepted as the theme and precise spirit of this Mass. In addition, the Introit may always serve to remind us, as we recall the sacred procession which it once accompanied, of the fundamental liturgical ideal and expectation of personal, individual, volitional participation in the entire sublime Action. Except on Palm Sunday, there is no longer a ritual procession which we can heartily join. Then let us as heartily bring these bodies and minds of ours to a most reverent and attentive and sincere participation in the

higher reality which, thank God, we do and always will have
— the Holy Sacrifice itself.

7. *Lord, have mercy . . . Christ, have mercy . . . Lord, have
mercy . . .* (the Kyrie of the Mass).

Since the prayers at the foot of the altar are the immediate
preparation of priest and people for the sublime action that
is the Mass, and since the Introit is the relic of the liturgical
procession of clergy and laity to the place of the Sacrifice,
there emerges a sense in which the Kyrie, the great cry for
mercy, stands as the initial prayer of the Mass itself.

As everyone understands, there is no divine decree as to
the precise language in which the Mass must be said; almighty
God is omnilingual. The language of the first Mass was
Aramaic; then Greek came into use; finally, in the Western
world, the tongue of both the Church and the Mass became
Latin. Throughout the first four Christian centuries the Holy
Sacrifice was offered only in the three languages of the in-
scription on the cross, but today the sacred Mysteries are
celebrated in 12 different tongues, including such languages as
Ethiopian, Armenian, and Coptic.

The Kyrie is the only Greek that remains in our Western
Mass. At the very least, this simple, eloquent plea ought to
give us modern Catholics a recurrent sense of the antiquity
or, better, the timelessness and universality of the faith which
we hold.

It is evident that the Kyrie is a Trinitarian prayer. It consists
of three sets of three invocations, the petition remaining always the same while the vocative changes as we address the
individual Persons of the blessed Trinity. We must recall a

point of earliest Christian usage which is emphatic in St. Paul: the Greek *Kyrios* is a strictly divine appellation. When we are told, as in Philippians, that *every tongue must confess Jesus Christ as the Lord, dwelling in the glory of God the Father,* there is no ambiguity about what Paul is saying: men must acknowledge the literal divinity of Christ. In the Kyrie God the Father is *Lord,* the Holy Spirit is *Lord,* and Christ is equated with the Father and the Holy Spirit.

This first petition of the Mass is generic, but it is unquestionably humble and lowly. As has so often been noted, Holy Mother Church never for an instant loses her balance in her dealings with Omnipotence; she never forgets that God is all and we are nothing. The creature can never afford to give himself airs and strut before the Godhead, treating the Creator as an equal, least of all on the threshold of the august Sacrifice of expiation for human sin. The repeated cry for mercy comes aptly in the forepart of the Mass.

Curiously, though, the Kyrie never conveys the impression of feebleness. It is a strong and mighty cry, and we need not doubt or question its sovereign power. It is worth an effort of the imagination to picture a dark day — which, please God, will never dawn — when not a single Mass would be offered in the whole round and circle of the earth. Hear for a fearful moment the desperate and ominous silence which would then take the place of the crashing chorus of *Kyrie eleison, Christe eleison, Kyrie eleison.* Is there anyone so rash and hardy as to suppose that such a black, blank day would not be, in the words of the funeral liturgy, *dies irae, dies miseriae et calamitatis, a day of wrath, a day of misery and calamity?*

We all wonder, periodically, what keeps our world functioning at all as it staggers drunkenly from crisis to crisis and reels stupidly (and willfully) from folly to ever more grotesque folly. Anyone may offer his own answer to the question. Perhaps it is the daily Sacrifice of the Mass, offered on so many altars in so many places, that holds our world together. Perhaps it is really because of each day's Kyrie that God does each day *have mercy on us.*

8.　*Glory to God in the highest. And on earth peace to men of good will* (from the Gloria of the Mass).

As is the case in so many details of the Mass ritual, the origin of the Gloria is obscure. When we first hear of this canticle in the liturgical Sacrifice it is reserved, like the triple blessing today, as a privilege for bishops only. Gradually the ordinary priest was permitted to say or sing the Gloria on special occasions; the initial strophe would suggest that the privilege may have been first extended for the Christ-Mass of the Nativity. In time the canticle became a fixed part of the ritual, though even today it is not always said.

The Gloria is a hymn, a song. It is a hymn of joyous praise. It is addressed to the Triune God.

Readers of St. Paul may occasionally have experienced surprise at the Apostle's repeated exhortation to sing. To the Colossians, for example, Paul says: *May all the wealth of Christ's inspiration have its shrine among you; now you will have instruction and advice from one another, full of wisdom, now there will be psalms, and hymns, and spiritual music, as you sing with gratitude in your hearts to God.*

We will not tarry over the manifest psychological and pedagogic benefits to be found not only in reciting together, but especially in singing together, our convictions or our hopes or our needs. Let us only observe that the Gloria is a very joyful song, and that the joy has two motives which are intimately connected: praise of God and, what Paul specifically mentions, gratitude.

Praise of God is a highly instructive form of prayer. Praise is expressed admiration; and when it is totally sincere and even joyful and wholly untinged with policy and solicitation, it argues both a notable degree of attachment to the one praised and a considerable unselfishness in the one praising. Like adoration, of which it is a part, the praise of God is prayer at its purest, and the Gloria is our noblest liturgical song of praise.

It is a splendid thing to voice our profound admiration of God our Lord, not so much for anything He has done — an entirely valid but different theme — as for what He is: *on account of Thy great glory.* The Gloria richly expresses this pure and grateful admiration in five successive phrases and three exalted titles addressed to God the Father; in four, and, later, three reverent addresses to God the Son, the Word Incarnate; and the prayer ends with a single strophe in honor of the Holy Spirit — a phrase, which for all its brevity, places the Third Person as coequal with the Father and the Son.

In the center of the Gloria, separating the two groups of titles given to the Word Incarnate, we discover a triple petition. The terms of the addresses here are borrowed from John the Baptist (it is good to hear the selfless precursor echoed in the hymn of praise) and from the Creed, but the petitions themselves could not be more generic. As we sincerely praise our most high God, we advert without detail to our constant, permanent need of His loving assistance in order that we may praise Him.

Since the Gloria is so thoroughly a canticle of joy, it is

omitted from all specifically penitential and sorrowful Masses, those Masses which are always known by their black or violet vestments. On every other occasion, however, we ought really to stir ourselves to join interiorly and more than verbally in the glowing tribute of loving, grateful admiration which Holy Mother Church pays to the Triune God thus early in the Holy Sacrifice. We cannot too often or too heartily remind ourselves that God our Lord is strictly all right; there's nothing wrong with *Him*.

9. *The Lord be with you. And with thy spirit* (the *Dominus vobiscum* of the Mass).

No less than eight times in the course of the Holy Sacrifice this greeting and response is exchanged between priest and people. In order to gain some insight into such an insistent procedure, let us recall two truths.

It cannot be too often repeated that the Christian religion is not an adjunct or a condiment to life; it *is* a life, a complete way of life. We sometimes do not notice that the Church, to use an easy but accurate phrase, has everything: she has a language of her own, a calendar of her own, a Food of her own, a tribunal of her own, a philosophy of her own, even a music that is distinctively hers. The Christian faith is supposed to penetrate and color and influence every action of every day; it should literally synchronize with every moment of our lives. As has been said, there is a Christian way of doing everything from getting up in the morning to going to bed at night, including work, play, reading, thinking, talking, commuting, and drinking beer.

It is not surprising, then, to find, as in the Pauline Epistles, that the early Christians used particular and particularly Christian greetings in encountering one another. The commonest form of the greeting seems to have been something like *Grace and peace be yours from God who is our Father and from the Lord Jesus Christ.* At the end of Galatians we read: *Brethren, the grace of our Lord Jesus Christ be with your spirit;* and the identical words occur at the close of Philippians. *With your spirit* is, of course, simply a refinement of "with you."

The other truth which is here pertinent is the communal or social nature of the Mass. Remember and remember again that the Holy Sacrifice is not a private and personal privilege or devotion of the ordained priest to which the faithful, if they are interested, may be admitted. The Sacrifice of the Mass is the exalted and characteristic daily liturgical action of the Mystical Body, and in that solid sense the Mass belongs and pertains just as much to the unlettered old lady in the last pew as to the reverend and perhaps learned and even perhaps holy priest at the altar.

This community and sharing and — exact word! — *cooperation* in the Mass is what is recalled every time the priest-celebrant addresses the attendant and attentive faithful. Observe that there is nothing to choose, so to speak, between the greeting and the response: *The Lord be with you. And with you, too.* There is a profound, most holy sense in which we are all not only one but one and equal in the Mass. I am a priest, but the Christ of the Mass is both yours and mine. The Victim that is sacrificed anew is both yours and mine. The grace of the Mass is for all of us. *Dominus vobiscum.*

A powerful conviction that the Mass belongs to each one of us, that it is a sublime action in which every one of us is deeply involved, should be part of the liturgical equipment of every earnest Catholic. There is that casual phrase, current nowadays, whereby we speak of "getting into the act." The expression is so accurate when it is reverently applied to our assisting at Mass. Whenever the priest says — and he is usually facing the people, then — *The Lord be with you,* let each one, as in his heart he answers *And with you, too,* bestir himself anew to get into the act. The act is the sacrificial offering of Christ to His Father. The act is the act of Calvary renewed. Willy-nilly, we are all of us involved. Let us be willingly, heartily, fervently involved.

Why should we not even borrow, upon occasion and for other uses, from the liturgy of the Mass? To the faithful readers of these lines the priestly scribe writes most truly: *Dominus vobiscum.*

10. *Let us pray. . . . Through our Lord Jesus Christ. . . . Amen* (the usual form of the collect or liturgical prayer of the Mass).

After the greeting to the people which follows the Gloria, the celebrant of the Mass turns to the right, or epistle, side of the altar, spreads his hands, bows slightly, and announces: *Oremus, Let us pray.* There ensues the collect or oration, as it is called, the first strictly petitionary prayer of the Mass.

It would not be at all surprising if a stranger to the liturgy of Holy Mother Church felt a distinct disappointment when first brought into contact with these Mass collects. (Incidentally, the original intent of this word is not clear. The reference is probably to the assembly of the faithful now gathered or *collected* together.) These prayers are always brief; they are always reserved, being cool and almost dry in tone; and although they are always petitionary, the graces or favors asked are not what one might possibly expect. Let us examine for a moment this petitionary side of the Church's inner life.

In the first place, the Mass petitions are notably generic rather than specific. Some who are wise in these deep matters think that when, originally, the priest at Mass said *Oremus,* there followed a little pause in which the faithful individually commended their needs to God. However that may be, the collect, although it implies and contains particular petitions (as the generic always implies and contains the specific), is never a particularized prayer. The Church here does not ask, on behalf of her children, for fair weather or cessation of headaches or high marks in examinations or a favorable diagnosis or that the appalling people next door may move away. Holy Mother Church, while entirely sympathetic to the immediate requirements of her needy and sorely tried and generally reasonable children, does not, of course, enshrine these immediate needs in her timeless liturgy — although, be it noted, she does have highly specific prayers for use on particular occasions.

No, the Mass petition is always very general, and is never exclusively temporal. For the most part Holy Mother Church prays in a kind of double-barreled or contrasting or at least parallel fashion, asking for A and then for B. So we hear supplications of this sort: *Make us despise what is worldly and love what is heavenly; free us from our sins and fill us with Your grace; look upon our weakness and protect us by Your might; shield us from adversity and keep us in peace;* and more of the same.

This cool, detached, low-keyed style in prayer does not at once appeal to colorful and intense personalities, but it can safely be asserted that the Church's way of praying steadily improves upon acquaintance. It is not spectacular, not emotional, not melodramatic. It runs under strict control; it is the exact opposite of sensationalism and hysteria. There is one sense in which the Church's prayer, if sincerely endorsed and intelligently employed, is always answered at once. It calms us.

In the larger sense, too, the Church's prayer is infallible, for Mother Church, illumined and guided by the Holy Spirit, infallibly asks for what, if we are at all cooperative, will infallibly be granted. Search as we will, we will never discover a liturgical petition of Holy Mother Church to which any conditional rider must be appended. This marvelous Mother of ours knows her Lord Christ, and she knows us. She knows how to talk to God, and what to ask on our behalf. Let us be convinced for once and for all: we are never wrong in our prayer when we pray as the Church prays.

In the collect for the third Sunday after Easter note the contrast: *reject . . . embrace.* Now let us pray this prayer. It asks for everything we need.

O God, to those who go astray You show the light of Your truth, that they may return to the way of salvation. Grant to all who profess themselves Christians that they may reject the things which are contrary to that name and embrace the things that are agreeable to it. Through our Lord Jesus Christ, Your Son, who is God, living and reigning with You in the unity of the Holy Spirit for ever and ever. Amen.

11. *You know this, my beloved brethren, well enough. It is for us men to be ready listeners . . .* (James 1:19; from the Epistle of the Fourth Sunday after Easter).

So often and so truly it has been said: the Church came forth from the womb of the synagogue. In that dawnlike age of Christianity which followed the first Christian Pentecost, the Apostles, as we see clearly from the Acts and the Pauline Epistles, continued to participate sincerely and unaffectedly in the worship service of the synagogue. It is evident that the earliest Christians did not conceive their religion as a break with Judaism but as the expected fulfillment thereof. So strong, indeed, was this assumption that the apostolic Church flirted briefly but dangerously with the idea that converts would have to submit not only to baptism but to circumcision.

It is not at all surprising, therefore, that the earliest Christian ritual borrowed without embarrassment from the ritual of the synagogue. Now one prominent feature of Jewish liturgy was the public reading of passages from Sacred Scripture. The Christians continued the practice, and, as was most natural, when the Christian group became conscious that they possessed their own unique sacred writings, they began publicly to read from these by preference, though by no means exclusively.

There was an even deeper reason for Christianizing the synagogue reading ritual. Nothing was more prominent in the early Christian consciousness than apostolicity: the need and the impulse and the obligation to teach. The solemn mandate which is enshrined in the closing verses of the Gospel of Matthew burned into the Christian heart and spirit: *You, therefore, must go out, making disciples of all nations, and baptizing them in the name of the Father, and of the Son, and of the Holy Ghost, teaching them to observe all the commandments which I have given you.* The Church perceived at once that the final member or precept of that sacred commission, the pedagogic task, was certainly not to be confined, for its object, to proselytes. The children of Mother Church are not initiated for once and for all; they must go on being taught, always.

The most explicit ritual teaching of the Church is achieved by the public reading of an Epistle and a Gospel in each Sunday Mass. Our good people ought to perceive sharply the inestimable difference, in deepest nature, between the Sunday Epistle-Gospel which they hear and perhaps read at Mass and the welter of *ad hoc* announcements which may also happen along.

As every Catholic knows from experience, the Sunday Epistle is generally much more difficult to follow and grasp than the Sunday Gospel. One reason for the difference might be that 42 of the 52 Sunday Epistles are taken from the letters of St. Paul, and St. Paul, who was a model in so many ways, is not always a model of clarity in expression. Still, such an animadversion is manifestly unfair, since the liturgical Gospel commonly possesses a completeness which enables it to stand on its own, as it were, whereas the liturgical Epistle is invariably wrenched from an epistolary context which it needs.

The solution to the problem of the Mass lesson would seem to be a kind of private lesson in advance. Good things (like Mass) are worth preparing for. A Saturday night or early Sunday morning reading of the Epistle of the day in its context, with perhaps a glance at a commentary of some sort, would make us more receptive pupils when Holy Mother Church proceeds to instruct us through her sacred liturgy.

Teaching is always such a two-sided thing. There must be one to teach, but there must be one also who is willing to learn. How apt and perceptive is St. James, for example, in the Epistle for the Fourth Sunday after Easter! *It is for us men to be ready listeners. . . .*

12. *Alleluia, alleluia. Christ has risen and His light has shone upon us whom He redeemed with His blood, alleluia. I came forth from the Father and have come into the world. Again I leave the world and go to the Father, alleluia* (intervening chant of the Mass for the Fifth Sunday after Easter).

Holy Mother Church in her liturgy freely makes use of certain sound principles of art, not, heaven knows, because the worship of the Divine Majesty is primarily a work of art, but because sound principles of art are rooted in that which the beatniks of every age fear and therefore abominate — sanity and common sense. For example, every art that is not diseased recognizes the imperative need of variety for the sake of relief; unvarying tension is always one of the marks of psychological imbalance. The Oriental mystic may sit like a graven image and, scarcely breathing, will repeat, no doubt with relish, the thousand names of God. But he does breathe — in, out, in, out — and the names are many, they are not one.

In the ancient Church a psalm was sung between the reading of the Epistle and the reading of the Gospel. The reason was simply the relief of which we speak. Listeners were many and readers were few in all past ages. Presumably the devout Christians at Mass really did listen with close and maybe hungry attention to the splendid, heartening, profound words of both Epistle and Gospel. It was good for the folk, in between the two hearings, to sing a little. These intervening chants, which have four technical names, Gradual, Tract, Alleluia, and Sequence, are noticeably repetitious, and we can easily guess why. The most satisfactory procedure in untrained group singing is for a couple of soloists (cantors) to sing the parts that change, and for all the eager bystanders (we mean *participants*) to join in the standard chorus.

The intervening chants sometimes refer directly to the event or feast that is being celebrated, but more often they simply but strongly echo the mood, the spirit of the feast. Frequently there is some anticipation here of what will be read and heard in the Gospel that is immediately to follow. It is good for us sons and daughters of Holy Mother Church to observe that even when the Church, in her ceremonial, seems most casual and transitional, she knows exactly what she is doing. She is at once the wisest and gentlest and most serious of teachers.

The complete hymn (Sequence) which may occur at this point is now heard only on very special feasts or occasions: Easter, Pentecost, Corpus Christi, the Seven Sorrows of Mary, the Requiem Mass. Rare as they are, these venerable songs richly merit the notice of all who wish to think and pray and live as the Church thinks and prays and lives. The *Veni Sancte Spiritus, Stabat Mater,* and *Dies Irae* are pure, exalted poetry in which undimmed theology is fellow to unabashed tenderness.

It will naturally occur to the Catholic mind as an objection that one can hardly be completely attentive to all the parts of the Mass on all occasions. The difficulty is valid. One fact is that the sacred liturgy contains a positive embarrassment of riches. Another fact is that poor old human concentration is unstable at best, and tends to waver (thank heaven) even when assaulted by the strident effrontery of television. Still, because we cannot attend closely to all the parts of the Mass all the time it does not follow that we cannot sharply heed some of the parts of the Mass some of the time. Let us come with simple, alert willingness to be taught and guided and (good word) edified. Mother Church and the Holy Spirit will take it from there.

13. *The Lord be with you. And with you, too. The continuation of the holy Gospel according to St. . . . Glory to Thee, Lord. At that time Jesus . . .* (introduction to the Gospel at every Mass).

Once, at a large assembly of priests here in the United States, the priest-secretary of the convention came hurrying to the stage of the meeting hall holding in his hand a sheet of yellow paper. He announced that the convention had received a cablegram from the Holy Father. Instantly, without suggestion, instruction, or signal, the entire throng rose to its feet. Nothing was remarked about the incident either then or afterward. It was instinctively clear to that audience of priests that they must stand at respectful attention as they listen to a direct message from their Supreme Pastor and beloved Holy Father.

When the Gospel is read at Mass the whole congregation comes to its feet. The action is the same one of reverence and respect. We stand at grave attention as we hear again the word of God about, or immediately from, the Word of God.

It is at the reading of the Gospel that in every Mass the teaching function of the Church reaches its explicit climax. Now Mother Church instructs us through her exalted Bridegroom Himself. And He teaches us *et factis et dictis: by the things He does and the things He says.*

What is the lesson that we needy children of Mother Church must learn in the repeated reading of the Gospel at Mass? The lesson to be learned is the noblest, highest, holiest, and best:

it is Christ Himself. It would be very wise for us to anticipate
the reading of the Gospel of the Mass by repeating earnestly
the significant petitionary formula of St. Ignatius Loyola:
"Lord Christ, I ask the grace, in the hearing of Your word,
to know You more intimately, that I may love You more
deeply, so that I will follow You more faithfully."

As everyone understands, the most effective mode of learning is not by abstract precept but from a living model. The
teacher who wants to introduce innocent children to the
perils of the alphabet does not lecture. She goes to the black-
board, takes a piece of chalk, and says simply: "Watch me."
In every Gospel Christ our Savior says to all of us both "Listen
to Me" and "Watch Me" — "Heed what I say; do as I do."
Here is the supreme Christian pedagogy.

In the artless, receptive manner of children who sorely need
to be instructed in their supernatural A B C's, we ought all to
listen to every Gospel. But as we listen, we must with God's
help engage in a rudimentary but sharp interior activity, which
alone will bring the gospel teaching to a point. Each one of
us must ask sincerely: "Where does this fit into *my* life?"

The answer to that question will not always be instantane-
ously clear. Yet upon occasion the really alarming gap between the gospel teaching and personal daily behavior will become apparent to any Christian who possesses the most fundamental honesty. To choose but a single example, the ex-
traordinary obtuseness of not a few Christian consciences with
regard to our Lord's primary doctrine of fraternal charity
would seem to suggest that some individuals never do hear the
Gospel when it is read. It is possible, of course, to quarrel bit-
terly with my family immediately before Mass and then to
resume the battle immediately after Mass and yet fulfill the
precept of assisting at Mass. But am I then paying any real

attention to Christ in the Gospel and Christ in the Mass?

14. *I believe in one God, the Father almighty . . . And in one Lord Jesus Christ . . . And in the Holy Spirit . . . (from the Creed as read in the Mass).*

The symbol of faith which we recite at Mass — and which, incidentally, brings to a close the first distinct portion of the ritual — is a summary or formula, and like every summary or formula, it is incomplete. The Catholic must and does believe in truths which are not mentioned here; one thinks immediately of the Assumption of our Lady. Yet a formula like the Creed is extremely useful. It reminds us regularly and conveniently of the basic tenets of our Catholic religion, and it could very well serve, much more than it does serve with most of us, as a most reliable handbook for that sane and commendable reflection which we term *meditation.*

The Creed, despite an evident Trinitarian form, may be regarded as falling into four sections or groups of articles. The general subject of belief in each portion is, in this order, God the Father, Christ the Word Incarnate, the Holy Spirit, and the Church. The division is significant. We do not, of course, believe *in* the Church as we believe *in* God, yet the faith which we profess *in* the Triune God is professed *within* the Church.

In the opening section of the Creed we proclaim our belief in the existence, the Fatherhood, the unicity of God, and in God as the Creator and origin of all things. So much and such fundamental doctrine in a few phrases! There are no wasted words in the Creed — which is one reason why it merits at least periodic close examination.

There follows an admirable summation of Christology. Note the striking insistence on our Lord's divinity even before we meet any mention of the Incarnation. We gratefully genuflect as we recall the blessed fleshing of the Word of God, and it is here, of course, that our Lady is forever enshrined in the symbol of faith. Next we bring to mind our Savior's sacrificial death, His triumphant resurrection, His ascension and solemn, eternal session at the side of His Father's majesty. Finally we state our conviction that this same Christ will someday return as supreme and absolute Judge of all mankind.

Part three declares the existence, the procession (from Father and Son), and the equal divinity of the Holy Spirit: *who with the Father and the Son is no less adored and glorified.* . . .

The closing section of the Creed contains four articles: belief in the true Church, in valid baptism, in final resurrection, and in immortality.

It would be desirable, naturally, if each of us at every Mass in which the Creed is said could be thoughtfully attentive to each article of the formula. Let us, however, be reasonable; let us not torture this poor, stumbling human intellect even under the excuse of religion. As we read the Creed on various occasions, our attention will be drawn more strongly to this point of faith or to that. Very good. But let us above all be consistently grateful for the Creed, not simply in the sense of being glad of the ready (and heady) formula, but in the larger sense of rejoicing in the gift of faith, of being glad beyond measure that we find it in our power and capacity honestly to recite the Creed.

Perhaps it is part of God's gift of faith to us that we do not actually see, as we recite the Creed, what a staggering act of credence is here demanded of us. *Credo* is a very big and brave and beautiful word — and fact.

II. THE OFFERTORY

15. *Return, Lord, save my life, rescue me because of Your kindness* (the Offertory Chant of the Mass for the Second Sunday after Pentecost).

The Mass is a single, coherent, organic act, or, more exactly, it is the actual representation of such a single act, the redemptive death of the Lord Christ. Nevertheless, the Mass has two distinct aspects. On one side the Mass is a sacrifice, on the other it is a meal. It seems clear that in the beginning it was the sacred eating aspect of the liturgical action that received the heavier emphasis. Very soon, however, the sacrificial dimension of the religious ceremony became the primary, though never the exclusive, consideration. The sacred action was a sacrificial action; the sacred meal that followed was a sacrificial meal.

The new emphasis gradually resulted in a liturgical ceremony which, regrettably, has not survived to our own day: the offertory procession. Whereas originally, as we see clearly from the First Epistle to the Corinthians, each Christian brought his own food for the communal supper which accompanied the celebration of the Eucharist, so now each one brought his gift of bread and wine to provide the material for the Eucharist sacrifice. The episcopal celebrant of the solemn Mass, assisted by priests, deacons, and subdeacons, received these gifts from the faithful who came in procession, chanting a psalm, for the presentation. When all the gifts had been accepted it was reasonable and necessary that the celebrant should wash his hands before proceeding with the sacred action. The offertory verse in our present Mass is the relic of the ancient procession chant. The ceremonial washing of the celebrant's fingers remains as part of the Mass today.

It may seem — again, regrettably — that the faithful no longer provide the necessary material elements for the sacrifice of the Mass. But they do. It is at this point in the sacred action that the collection is taken up. At first glance this would appear to be an ill-chosen moment for the gathering of money. In fact, the moment is wisely and significantly chosen. The collection is the modern equivalent of the offertory procession. The change may not in every way represent an improvement, but it is not senseless, it is not gross, it is not unfeeling. The liturgical offertory is the time for liturgical offerings.

A liturgical offering. It would be genuinely constructive if the generous Catholic layman thus truly regarded the contribution which he makes at Mass. The layman should provide his Sunday offering — and to the honest limit of his capacity — in order to make possible, though it be in the widest, most inclusive sense, the sacrifice of the Mass. Not only must bread and wine be purchased if there is to be Mass, but there must be a considerable quantity of altar equipment, all of which must be renewed, laundered, kept in fitting condition. The priests, without whom, despite all their unworthiness, there can be no Mass, must be maintained, and new, young, eager priests must be carefully, thoroughly formed. The church itself must be so kept that it will be as little unworthy as possible to be the scene and shelter of Calvary renewed.

These are the reasons why the openhearted and open-handed Catholic layman gladly plays his part in the contemporary substitute for the offertory procession. Let this good man be religious and liturgical even as he puts his hand in his pocket.

It must have been a deep satisfaction, in the olden time, for people to know that the bread they had baked and the wine they had pressed would serve so lofty a purpose as to become the Body and Blood of Christ, and thus return to the givers. But the situation is not essentially changed; indeed, it may even be more wonderful, now. Can anyone think of a better use for gross coin than that to which it is put every Sunday at the offertory of the Mass? Here is my dollar. Let the priest buy the necessary bread and wine. Let him do with those elements what only he, by the power of the Holy Spirit, can do. Let him give me back my gift — in Holy Communion.

16. *Accept, holy Father, almighty and eternal God, this spotless host . . .* (prayer at the offering of the bread in the Mass).

During that introductory section of the Mass which was anciently the Mass of the Catechumens, the celebrant, in a certain sense, does nothing. This entire portion of the sacred ritual consists simply of prayers and readings. Now, at the Offertory, the proper sacrificial act begins. The priest removes the veil from the chalice, lifts before him in both hands the paten or gold plate holding the disc of food, and offers to God the gift of bread: *Accept, holy Father, almighty and eternal God, this spotless host. . . .*

Our attention is immediately drawn to the ritual description of the offering. We do not beg God graciously to accept "this bread," but *this spotless host*. The word *host,* in liturgical usage, means *victim: O salutaris hostia* is *O saving Victim.* Hence this presentation prayer is distinctly anticipatory. We offer to the divine Majesty not only what the gift is at the moment, but, even more, what it will shortly and wonderfully be.

It is genuinely significant that mankind, in its historical effort to give a present to its God (and even to its gods), has inclined to choose as the gift either a living object like a bullock or a sheep or a pigeon (or a human being), or some kind of food. Food, one realizes, was once living material; food ministers to life. There seems to be a religious instinct whereby the living man feels impelled to offer a living object as a gift to the living God by whom, finally, man and all that is vital live.

Thus, in the Mass the gift to God of bread and wine is not in itself an offering to be despised. Yet the thought of the Church leaps at once from the food that is to the Food that will be, from the poor gift of the present moment to the sublime, exalted Gift that will shortly be lifted up to the *holy Father, almighty and eternal God.* By anticipation, the offertory bread represents the blameless Victim whose priceless death is sacramentally renewed in every Mass.

The prayer of offering specifies two of a number of possible reasons or intentions which underlie the religious act of sacrifice. The gift is seen first in its expiatory function, for it is offered in atonement for *sins, offenses, and negligences.* Very notable here is the emphasis on the priest's own unworthiness, his own need for forgiveness and expiation. Next, the gift is offered in large petition: not only *for all here present,* but also *on behalf of all faithful Christians living and dead, that for me and for them it may be a means of salvation unto life everlasting.* The simple, touching prayer looks both backward and forward in both time and need.

The need, or at least the thing desired in the offertory moment, is the identification, conscious and fully volitional, of the offerer with the offering. And it must be understood clearly, for once and for all, that the one who offers the

Mass is not merely or only the celebrant, though the priest is, in all his unworthiness, the absolutely essential agent of the sacrifice. The offerer of the Mass is the Church, and the Church consists of Christ, the priest, and the Christian community. Everyone who is present offers the Mass.

Every time the priest, at Mass, uncovers the chalice and takes the paten in his hands, every person in the church ought to think: "The bread is being offered to God. By anticipation, Christ is being offered to God. In sober reality — but depending, of course, on my interior disposition — *I* am being offered to God. Amen. So be it. *Accept, holy Father . . .*"

17. *God, who has established the nature of man in wondrous dignity and even more wondrously has renewed it . . .* (prayer of the Mass as wine and water are poured into the chalice).

After the offering of the bread the celebrant of the Mass moves to the right corner of the altar. There he pours into the chalice a quantity of wine and adds a few drops of water. The duality of these elements and their mingling provide the key to the profound and eloquent prayer which accompanies the action.

Holy Mother Church speaks unhesitatingly about the *wondrous dignity* of human nature as created by God. The truth is important. Creation does not represent a lapse or a concession or a failure on the part of the omnipotent Creator; human nature is not evil.

There is a black, unmitigated pessimism which is often enough attributed to Christian, Catholic thought and which, in fact, is utterly foreign to it. Man is like a worm, but he is not a worm. Man can be beastly, but he is not a beast. Man becomes, upon occasion, contemptible, but he is not contemptible. He possesses intrinsic and authentic *dignity,* a *dignity* that is simply *wondrous.* He is made in the image and likeness of God Himself. He can accommodate all creation and even, to a degree, infinity within his skull by the miracle of intellect, and he is godlike in the freedom of his will. Man, unlike any ape or amoeba, can thank God for the gift of being and can love God for creating him. Dignity means worth. There actually is a sense in which man, by divine gift, is worthy of God.

This is the worth that man destroyed by the original sin. The *wondrous dignity* of God's adopted son was soiled and shattered — hopelessly and forever, one would have said. But then the merciful Lord of all *even more wondrously . . . renewed it.* To the marvel of creation there succeeded the larger marvel of redemption. There is scarcely to be found in human thought an optimism which can compare with that of Holy Mother Church. She sadly regards the fall of man as the worst of all possible disasters. And then she calmly describes that crime, which occasioned the blessed redemption, as *felix culpa: happy fault.*

The second duality which is here mentioned (for this prayer is all pairs) is that of humanity and divinity. We ask *that through the mystery of this water and wine we may be made partners of His divinity who has become partaker of our humanity.* The petition seems daring in the extreme, but, as a piece of theology, it is entirely sound and discreet.

The Second Person of the adorable Trinity came among us and literally assumed *our humanity* in order to redeem us. Now redemption meant and means a restoration — the essential restoration of man to the state of supernatural elevation which he had lost by his sin. But that supernatural state signified precisely an actual though mysterious sharing by man, whose own nature is only human, in the very nature of God, who is divine. When, therefore, the Son of God became *partaker of our humanity,* it was in order to make us once more *partners of His divinity.* Such quasi-deification seems a great deal to ask or expect. But there it is. Or rather, for anyone in sanctifying grace, here it is.

It is at the Offertory, of course, that the Person of Christ our Savior, the God-Man, enters more explicitly into our thought at Mass. Now, as mere bread and wine are being ritually prepared for what, in the infinite goodness of God, they will become, we may well begin to think more closely of this loving, gentle, magnificent Redeemer of ours to whom we owe so much and who has so intimately associated Himself with us. Let our honest, unemotional desires turn to Him. He has indeed *become partaker of our humanity.* Let us will most heartily to *be made partners,* in high degree, *of His divinity.*

18. *We offer You, Lord, the cup that brings salvation. We beg of Your mercy that it may ascend as a sweet fragrance before Your divine Majesty, for our salvation and for that of the whole world* (the prayer, in the Mass, at the offering of the wine).

The Mass is the religious act of sacrifice, and the religious act of sacrifice involves the giving of a material gift to God. What is given to God in the Mass is, at the outset, bread and wine; but these objects are never regarded simply as bread and wine. The gifts we offer are not considered, liturgically, as what they are, but always with an eye to what they will be. At the offering of the bread we speak not of bread but of *hostia,* a *victim.* At the offering of wine we mention not wine but *calicem salutaris,* a *cup of salvation.* What we mortal men bring to the altar is pedestrian and little worthy of the divine notice. But what the power of Christ will make of our poor presents is overwhelming. Our bread and wine become the only gift that is truly and actually and completely worthy of the divine Majesty.

The sacrifice of the Mass has, therefore, a dual aspect which is immensely consoling. The Mass is pleasing to God. The Mass is salutary or beneficial for men.

From the initial fact that the Mass is a sacrifice it would follow that the Mass is pleasing to God. The act of sacrifice, by which the divine nature and absolute dominion of God are recognized and by which man symbolically offers himself entirely to God, is manifestly the proceeding of all proceedings which is most truly religious — most fitting and proper for God, most becoming for man.

Even more pertinent, however, is the added and special fact that in *this* sacrifice, which inevitably meant the end of all other sacrifices, the Victim that is offered to God is the only victim that is or could be supremely worthy of God. Twice in the earthly lifetime of Christ our Lord the heavens opened and the voice of the eternal, omnipotent Father was heard in joyous affirmation: *This is My beloved Son, in whom I am well pleased.* That same Son is the priceless Victim who is offered and immolated in every Mass. At every Mass, every church or chapel from cathedral to mission hut rings and echoes with that same proud affirmation and acceptance by God the Father.

As for men, the value and benefit of the Mass for them may readily be calculated, in so far as it is not incalculable, from a curious but indisputable historical fact. Whenever and wherever Catholic people are deprived of the Mass, within a hundred years the Catholic faith of those people is either corrupt or dead.

There is a deep, subtle, altogether intimate connection of the most practical sort between the Catholic Mass and the Catholic faith. So it is that the Catholic who truly loves the Mass is the best kind of Catholic. So it is that the Catholic who is indifferent to the Mass and regularly absent from it is dangling perilously, though he knows it not, on the very edge of his faith. So it is that we recognize the ultimate meaning and value of the priest. The priest is important, not because he is eloquent or pious or hardworking or kindly or competent or learned, though all these he ought, indeed, to be. The priest is important because the priest means the Mass. The secret law of Catholicism is this: no priest, no Mass; no Mass, finally no faith. It is with a sure and religious instinct that Catholics love their priests.

With wonder and astonishment we reflect that by one and the same act a fallible, mortal man may even daily pay infinite honor to God and do immeasurable good for himself. Is it surprising that Catholics are found at Mass when no law says they must be there?

19. *In a humble spirit and with a contrite heart may we be accepted by You, Lord, and may our sacrifice so be offered in Your sight this day as to please You, Lord God* (prayer at Mass after the offering of the chalice).

The gifts of bread and wine have been ritually offered to almighty God. The celebrant of the Mass now bows toward the altar (which always symbolizes Christ), and, joining his

hands and resting them lightly on the altar table, he recites
the significant prayer that we have here quoted. The priest
does not now ask that the material and tangible gifts be
acceptable to God; no, but *may we be accepted by You, Lord*.
In other words, the gift of bread and wine, like every gift,
means something more than appears.

The rationalization of that absolutely universal and timeless
practice, gift giving, is not simple. There are not a few reasons
for making a gift, ranging from the strictly pragmatic (the
firm hope of getting something in return) to the almost
completely pure (as is generally the case in anonymous bene-
factions). Always, however, the gift possesses an invisible
suggestion or symbolism: it conveys some significance beyond
itself. At best, the present genuinely symbolizes the one who
brings it; it represents his high regard, his authentic love,
his earnest devotedness to the offering's recipient. The gift,
in short, stands for the giver.

There is a sense in which we may say that bread and wine
hold no interest for the divine Majesty. What interests God
our Lord about these objects is, first, what they will become,
and, second, what they signify. The offering of our gifts in
the Mass can mean no less than the offering of ourselves.
May we be accepted by You, Lord.

But then, what does it mean to offer one's self to God?
Do we meet here a purely ceremonial gesture, or do these
words of the Mass stand for a reality?

When a human being sincerely offers himself to almighty
God, he surely presents his person and whole being as ready
and eager for whatever use God may wish to make of him.
If the act of self-oblation does not mean that, then it is hard
to see what it does mean. Such oblation is, of course, always
understood in terms of the individual's state and capacity.

When a husband and father offers himself to God in the Mass, it does not mean that he will forthwith abandon his happy, mortgaged home for the nearest monastery. In the simplest terms, when we offer ourselves genuinely to God, we undertake to do God's will.

Doing God's will has two aspects. It means obedience to God's law, and it means acceptance of what God sends.

It is very evident that at this point there begins to appear what is never grasped by those who do not understand the Mass: the strong, positive, operative connection between the Mass and daily life.

As the Catholic leaves the church after Mass, he stands committed, during the period until his next Mass, to obey God's known law in all its details, and to receive humbly and patiently, as from God's hands, whatever this day or this period will bring. One sees immediately that the oftener a Catholic assists at Mass and thus renews the commitment involved, the more apt he will be to live up to the commitment.

The earnest offering of one's self to anyone or anything is never exactly easy. Self-dedication is scarcely as convenient and comfortable as self-seeking. Still, when we are reminded, as every Mass does indeed remind us, of the total self-oblation of God's own Son as that oblation was dreadfully achieved on Calvary, we must feel considerably less reluctant to follow through after we have said with the priest, *may we be accepted by You, Lord.*

20. *Come, Sanctifier, almighty and eternal God, and bless this sacrifice prepared for the glory of Your name* (invocation after the offering of the bread and wine in the Mass).

The elements of the ritual sacrifice are duly prepared and ready. The small circlet of bread and the cup of wine have been presented to the divine Majesty and now rest on the corporal, that square of linen upon which the intimacies of the Mass take place. Through the priest, the accredited agent of the sacrifice, the offerers have presented themselves to God, begging that they may be acceptable to the omnipotent Lord of all. The celebrant of the mysteries makes a particular gesture. Lifting his eyes, he raises his parted hands in a circle, joining them at the top of the arc; then, with his right hand he blesses the offerings. During all this he is reciting the invocation which is our present text.

Who is addressed in this invocation? Almighty God, of course. But is the prayer more specifically directed to the Third Person of the blessed Trinity? It would appear so. In old manuscripts the words *Holy Spirit* are found after *Sanctifier*. Besides, this short petition is the Western or Roman parallel to a solemn supplication which, in the Eastern liturgies, occurs *after* the consecration and which is accorded distinct prominence. In the liturgy of St. John Chrysostom the prayer is worded thus:

> We offer unto Thee this reasonable and unbloody sacrifice, and we call on Thee, we pray Thee and beseech Thee, send down Thy Holy Spirit upon us and upon these gifts here present. And make this bread the precious body of Thy Christ, and that which is in the chalice the precious blood of Thy Christ, changing them by Thy Holy Spirit.

There is in traditional Christian belief and terminology a way of thinking and speaking about God our Lord whereby certain divine activities are referred more particularly to one Person of the Trinity. Thus we think of the Father as Creator, the Son as Wisdom, the Holy Spirit as the indwelling Guest of the soul in sanctifying grace. So also a theologian like Msgr. Romano Guardini describes the Christian life as a journey, God the Father being the goal, the Son being, as He Himself affirmed, the way, the Holy Spirit being the leader. The technical theological term for this process of reference is *appropriation*.

With regard to our present text the eminent liturgist Father Pius Parsch writes:

> In this prayer the Church expresses her conviction of faith that just as the Holy Spirit (by appropriation) was the Author of the human body of Christ — *Et incarnatus est de Spiritu Sancto, ex Maria Virgine* (*And He became man by the Holy Spirit, from the Virgin Mary*) — so He is also the Author of the real presence of the body of Christ in the Eucharist.

One is sometimes struck — and the word is apt — by that clipped liturgical imperative, *Veni, Come.* In the Advent liturgy the terse expression is steadily addressed to the Word Incarnate, but otherwise, when it occurs ritually, the sharp cry, which certainly suggests urgency, is invariably uttered to the Holy Spirit. We beg the Spirit of God not to be far off, but to approach us, draw near us, enter into us, so that there may be achieved in us that actual interior transformation which is needful if creature and Creator are to be in fact united, made one, in love.

Come, Sanctifier, we pray in the Mass, *and bless this sacrifice. . . .* But, as has been said, that which is offered in the Holy Sacrifice is not only Christ, but, through and in and with Christ, ourselves. *Come,* then, *Sanctifier, and bless,* enrich, transform the least worthy element in *this sacrifice; bless* us, priest and people, together.

We think of the Holy Spirit as the all-wise and all-powerful ruler and moderator of the whole vast world of the supernatural. Indeed, He is so wise and powerful that He can and does mightily influence every single, smallest factor in that tremendous world. For example, me in this Mass.

21. *With the pure in heart I will wash my hands clean, and take my place among them at Your altar, listening there to the sound of Your praises, telling the story of all Your wonderful deeds* (Ps. 25:6–7 — the *Lavabo* in the Mass).

As is well known, the celebrant of the Mass in the ancient ritual washed his hands after the Offertory for the same prosaic reason that a bishop today does the identical thing after anointing in confirmation and holy orders — in order to wash his hands. In the course of receiving from the faithful their humble, sincere gifts of bread and wine (and, as we shall see, other things) during the offertory procession, the celebrant's hands had become necessarily soiled. Before proceeding with the sacrifice, he performed a simple ablution.

It stands to reason, however, that the obvious symbolism of the hand washing could never have been absent from the Christian mind. Men have always been profoundly convinced of the necessity for some kind of ritual purity, or at least purification, in their solemn dealings with divinity. There has probably never been a religion without lustrations (washings). We know from the Gospels how particular the Pharisee of Christ's day was about hand washing, and the now celebrated Dead Sea scrolls have made it clear that elaborate ablutions figured largely in the monkish life at Qumran. John the Baptist seized on this act as the trademark of his movement and apostolate.

So, very early, the washing of hands in the Mass was accompanied by the recitation of appropriate verses from Psalm 25, verses which both mentioned and begged for interior purity of heart. *Be it mine to guide my steps clear of wrong; deliver me in Your mercy.*

It is hardly necessary to observe that the purity of heart demanded by dealings and intimacy with almighty God is far more comprehensive than even the considerable virtue involved in Christian chastity. For example, *the pure in heart* are marked by such pronounced Christian virtues as fraternal charity.

We may notice here what we will observe again, that by an odd paradox love of neighbor is at once a major effect of the Eucharist and one of the major requirements in order that the Eucharist may be most effective. Too often we regard our Holy Communion and our assistance at Mass as individual and even private activity rather than as strongly communal actions. The altar rail is really meant to be a table, the extension of the altar table; and at this family table the Christian community gathers in oneness for its holy sacrifice and its holy food. Strife and bitterness ill become a true family, and as the priest washes his hands in the Mass, we may well and once again purge our hearts, at least by sincere renunciation, of all harshness and anger and resentment.

That word *renunciation* suggests another element in Christian purity of heart. We all urgently want many things because we all honestly (for the most part) need many things. But wanting things, not in the exact sense of lacking them but in the more common sense of longing and pining and fretting for them, can become a disease. It will always be difficult for Christians to be Christian in the way of fixing the heart and its desires first on God and then on things, even when those things appear to us to be strict necessities. Our Savior has unequivocally told us: *Make it your first care to find the kingdom of God, and His approval, and all these things shall be yours without the asking.*

Of course, it continues to be laborious to achieve such Christian detachment. Let us not stop trying, however. As the priest, murmuring the purgative prayer, washes his hands, let us also make a brave new attempt to purge the heart of its painful longing for this, that, and the other. Mass would be so much more wonderful if, during it, we thought more about what we are giving to God and less about what we hope to get from God.

It only takes a moment to wash the fingers, but it takes — oh, how long it takes to wash the heart! Very well. Let us, God helping, get on with it.

22.   *Receive, Holy Trinity, this offering which we make to You in rememberance of the passion, resurrection, and ascension of our Lord Jesus Christ, and in honor of the blessed Virgin Mary* . . . (prayer of offering after the *Lavabo* of the Mass).

Returning to the center of the altar after the ritual washing of his fingers, the celebrant of the Mass bows low over the altar table and recites a prayer which merits our attention. It is a prayer of offering, of remembrance, of intercessory petition.

The stress here rests not on God's acceptance of our gifts, though that is what is asked, but on one of the motives for the offering which we make. According to St. Luke's account of the institution of the Eucharist, our Savior, after He had said, *This is My body, which is to be given for you,* immediately added, *do this for a commemoration of Me.* The Pauline version, in First Corinthians, is even more emphatic: *Take, eat; this is My body, which is to be given for you. Do this for a commemoration of Me. And so with the cup, when supper was ended, This cup, He said, is the new testament, in My blood. Do this, whenever you drink it, for a commemoration of Me. So it is the Lord's death that you are heralding, whenever you eat this bread and drink this cup, until He comes. . . .*

A prime reason, therefore, for the celebration and reception of the Eucharist is remembrance: that in and through this exalted sacrifice we may not for an instant forget but always most vividly remember the Lord Christ. And what we are to remember, above all else about Him, is *the Lord's death.* But Paul himself never separates the death of Christ from the victory of Christ, for these are but twin phases of the same supreme event. So, in this prayer of the Mass we renew our offering *in remembrance of the passion, resurrection, and ascension of our Lord Jesus Christ.* The Ascension is, of course, the completion of the Resurrection as the Resurrection is the completion of our Savior's death. St. Paul's expression is succinct: *So it is the Lord's death that you are heralding —* proclaiming, publishing, crying out — *whenever you eat this bread and drink this cup, until He comes.*

One might wonder how Christians could ever forget their Lord and all that He has done for them. We recall, in all reverence, Hamlet's agonized cry to his father's ghost:

> Remember thee?
> Ay, thou poor ghost, while memory holds a seat
> In this distracted globe. Remember thee?

And yet — well, fallen human nature is capable of incredible lapses as far as grateful remembrance is concerned. Indeed, we will never forget Christ as a living, present reality and Person — but thanks largely to the Holy Eucharist both as sacrament and sacrifice.

And in honor of the blessed Virgin Mary. . . . Again the liturgy speaks in the full consciousness of the communion of saints. The holy ones invoked here are, with the exception of the archangel Michael, the saints who were mentioned in the *Confiteor,* and even the order of naming them is the same. Our Lady stands first, as always, but let us notice in what liturgical esteem John the Baptist is held. Someday popular piety will rediscover heroic John; the liturgy never forgets him.

We ask the intercession of the saints that our sacrifice *may avail to their honor and our salvation.* In those few words we recognize a satisfactory exposition of the Roman Catholic practice, explicitly rejected by Protestantism, of invoking the saints. We really do not confuse even the holiest humanity with divinity. We address ourselves to God's favored friends simply and amply for their honor and our salvation. We are persuaded that they will *intercede for us in heaven, whose memory we celebrate on earth.*

The holy sacrifice of the Mass is not merely an elaborate memorial service. But it is, thank God, a most powerful and effective daily reminder of holy realities which we must never forget.

23. *Pray, brothers, that my sacrifice and yours may be acceptable to God the Father almighty* (the *Orate Fratres* of the Mass).

The Offertory is drawing to a close. All preparations are now complete. The elements of the sacrifice have been ritually set forth; the gifts have been reverently presented to God; the bread and wine await their ineffable transformation. The celebrant of the Mass turns to face the assembly of God's people. What is now said is not, indeed, addressed immediately and directly to the congregation, for the priest is speaking here to the ministers who, in the archetypal solemn Mass, would be his assistants in the offering of the sacrifice. Nevertheless, and particularly in the concrete circumstances of the more usual low Mass, it is difficult to see why the attendant faithful must be considered as excluded from the brief, earnest plea which the priest makes at this point. We will suppose, therefore, that at least by implication the celebrant of the Mass now begs all present to pray.

For what, in particular? That God may be pleased by the sacred action that is being performed, and may graciously accept the sacrifice. But notice how that action is now designated by the celebrant: *my sacrifice and yours.*

There is a valid sense in which the Mass belongs to the priest who celebrates it. Ever since the sorry scandals that occasioned the sorry Reformation, Mother Church has been notably sensitive on the subject of simony, the buying and selling of holy things. Yet the Church calmly allows a priest to accept and to retain as his own any offering that may be made to him when he celebrates Mass for a particular intention or at an individual request. As we all know, whenever any priest says Mass it is the whole living, mystical Christ that offers the sacrifice. Yet it remains as true that this Mass offered by this priest is this priest's Mass. Set side by side with priests, millionaires are poor fellows.

But — *my sacrifice and yours.* By what right do we read into these ritual words the suggestion that the Mass belongs also to all the faithful who are present?

The Holy Sacrifice belongs to the laity in a sense so rudimentary that we almost hesitate to advert to it. For the liturgical act of sacrifice a surprising quantity of — well, of material equipment, is necessary. There ought to be a church of sorts. There must be an altar, candles, a very special kind of book (ponderous, as any altar boy will attest), a chalice, bread and wine, a wide variety of vestments and linens, together with any number of incidental or occasional items like flowers and incense and music. Finally, to employ these materials at all fittingly there must be a trained and fairly well educated priest. Now, who provides all this? Who buys the vestments and the missal and the bread and wine? Who pays for the building and maintaining of both church and seminary? The laity, of course. There is a way in which the quiet, attentive layman in the pew makes every Mass possible. With justice, the celebrant of the Mass might think of him when he speaks of *my sacrifice and yours.*

In a deeper, more theological sense, too, the laity who may be present are involved in the Mass. What transpires at the altar is no private transaction between the priest and God. The Epistle to the Hebrews describes a priest as one *chosen from among his fellow men, and made a representative of men in their dealings with God,* precisely that he may *offer gifts and sacrifices in expiation of their sins.* So, at Mass, the man who was a layman before he was a priest acts now not only for himself, but also on behalf of *his fellow men,* and offers their Christ to their God as their sacrifice *in expiation of their sins.*

This is the reason, and not mere display or evident psychology, for the participation of the laity in the sacrifice of the Mass. The layman should play his part in the ritual action not by invitation or courtesy, but because he has, or rather is, a living, drastic part in and of the ritual action.

24. *May the Lord receive the sacrifice from your hands, for the praise and glory of His name, likewise for our benefit and for that of His holy Church* (the response, in the Mass, to the *Orate Fratres* of the celebrant).

The liturgical response to the priestly exhortation, *Pray, brothers,* begins with the Latin word *Suscipiat* and is well known among altar boys as a formidable mouthful of Latin. Any boy who knows and recites the *Suscipiat* without distortion is an acolyte indeed. In sense, the prayer is simplicity itself, for it is only a renewed expression of hope that God our Lord will graciously accept the sacrifice that is being offered. We may note, however, the two parts of the prayer.

May the Lord receive the sacrifice from your hands. The priest has just addressed the ministers of the Mass and, in some sort and by implication, the congregation, associating them with himself in the sacred action. The respectful answer of the acolyte stresses the unique function of the priest in the Mass: *from your hands,* says the server, the sacrifice will be received by the divine Majesty. Both emphases are just, of course. The whole Christian assembly offers the sacrifice with the priest, but there can be no sacrifice without the priest.

It is one thing to ask the faithful to appreciate the dignity of the priest; it is another and more urgent thing to ask the priest to appreciate his own dignity. Even the expressions we must use are misleading, for this sort of task always sounds as if the considerable importance of Father X actually had something to do with X. It hasn't. The laity are (or ought to be) sick and tired of deferring to Father because Father is a very positive man or because he works hard or is clever or because his car is bigger and better than most. The dignity of the priest may properly be described as Eucharistic. Nothing can absolutely destroy that dignity once a human being is given the awful power of changing bread and wine into the body and blood of Christ. Nevertheless, the priestly dignity waxes or wanes exactly as the individual priest is more or less Eucharistic in his life. Some one of these days a number of us well-meaning clerics are going to realize, perhaps with a start, precisely what — no, *who* — is permanently over there in the church.

The *Suscipiat* next recalls two most general reasons or intentions for which every Mass is offered.

Before there is question of anything else, the Mass is offered to God for the honor of God: *for the praise and glory of His name.* From this strict point of view it is impertinent to ask whether or not the Catholic as he goes to Mass on Sunday derives any good from so doing. Very few Catholics, and only those of a very queer stripe, would doubt that they gain by assisting at Mass; yet such profit is not the first reason for assistance. The primary task of the creature, always and everywhere, is to pay due honor to his Creator, and the Mass is the perfect way of discharging that obligation.

However: *likewise for our benefit and for that of His holy Church.* The Latin word which is here translated *benefit* is *utilitas.* We ask that the Mass may be *useful,* both for the members of this immediate community and for the entire vast family of the Church. To say that something is useful is to say that it is practical. And *practical* means "related to daily practice or doing or action."

With all reverence we observe that the holy sacrifice of the Mass is or ought to be a supremely practical reality. That is to say, the Mass at which we assist in the morning ought to exercise an influence over the rest of the day. Earnest Catholics must earnestly ponder this idea and problem of the effects of Mass when Mass is over. It is not easy, of course, to keep the supernatural operating throughout the highly natural day. Still, might we not at least advert to the possibility that what we do and say at Mass during one half-hour of the day might have some connection with what we do and say in all the other half-hours of the day?

25. *Look kindly, we beg You, Lord, on the gifts which we lay upon the holy altar, so that they may win Your mercy for us, and thus give honor to Your name* (the Secret of the Mass for the Twelfth Sunday after Pentecost).

After addressing to his associates in the Mass the exhortation, *Pray, brothers,* the celebrant of the Mass does himself pray. In accordance with extremely ancient liturgical procedure, the priest recites a prayer which is oddly called the *Secreta* (Secret), and which, not so oddly, is said in a tone so low that it is audible only to the priest himself.

There is only conjecture as to the origin and meaning of the term *Secreta.* We cannot now tell whether this prayer was called the Secret because it was recited in a low tone, or whether it was recited in a low tone because it was called the Secret. We are not certain whether to understand with *Secreta* the noun *oratio* (prayer) or the noun *ecclesia* (assembly, community, Church), in which latter case the prayer would be that of the inner, initiate Church as distinct from the earlier prayer of the *ecclesia collecta,* the complete assembly that included the catechumens or candidates for baptism.

What seems certain is that the present prayer — and in this it is sharply different from the early collect — is definitely an *oratio super oblata, a prayer over the offerings.* There is

scarcely a Secret to be found in the liturgy that does not
explicitly refer to the gifts or the mysteries or the sacrifice.
To this reference there is always added a petition.

Invariably, the Secret asks in one way or another that the
sacrifice may actually achieve its proper effects. By studying
the Secret in various Masses we would discover, and find
expressed with rich variety, what Holy Mother Church thinks
the holy sacrifice of the Mass ought to do for us.

Here are some samples of the petitions embodied in the
Secret of Sunday Masses. We ask, for instance, *that by virtue
of this sacrifice our daily life on earth may grow like that of
heaven.* Again, *that the offerings of each to the glory of Your
name may profit all alike for salvation.* Or, *by the power of
Your grace may these holy mysteries sanctify our lives in this
world and bring us to the joys that are eternal.* Lastly, let us
record two complete Secrets: *May these sacrifices, Lord, which
You have appointed to be offered for the glory of Your name,
so be made holy that they may become a remedy for all our
ills.* And, *Look mercifully upon our devoted service, we beg
You, Lord, that the gifts we offer You may be acceptable to
You, and for us be a support in our weakness.*

It is not difficult to detect a common denominator in these
Secret petitions. To begin with, there is repeated mention of
the basic dual intent of the sacrifice, the glory of God and the
good of man. The good of man is likewise specified according
to its double aspect as we plead for grace now and joy forever.
Finally, the grace we need now is both positive and negative:
holiness or steady growth in Christian virtue, and strong
protection against evils that threaten.

Reading these Secrets (and we have noted so few out of
so many), one does not know whether to marvel more at the
quiet wisdom of Mother Church or at the mighty power that

is evidently contained in the holy Sacrifice. Perhaps we all wonder at times why the Mass and Holy Communion do not do more for us, spiritually, than they seem to do. However, let us recall that supernatural growth is notoriously difficult to measure. All transcendental bookkeeping had best be left to the Holy Spirit. There is one calculation, though, which any moderately honest person might undertake. If (let me say paternally of myself) this is what I am after so many Masses and Holy Communions, what in this fallen world would I now be without them?

We will surely spend a portion of eternity being glad that we asked for what we ask for in the Secret of the Mass.

III. THE CANON

26. *The Lord be with you. And with your spirit. Lift up your hearts. We have them lifted up to the Lord. Let us give thanks to the Lord our God. It is meet and just* (introduction to the Preface, which is the introduction to the Canon of the Mass).

We come now to the heart and center of the Mass. We approach the consummation of the sacrifice.

The word *canon* is of Greek origin, and the basic notion involved is that of measure or rule. Hence our borrowed English term implies a norm or standard; we speak of canons of art, of taste. The Canon of the Mass is the absolutely fixed, standard, unchanging, essential portion of the sacrificial liturgy.

The Consecration is, of course, the center of the Canon of the Mass. Likewise, as has been widely observed, the Consecration is the exact center of an extraordinarily symmetrical liturgical construction.

On one side of the Consecration there is the Last Supper narrative, on the other side a memorial prayer of the Passion, Resurrection, and Ascension of our Lord. Just before the narrative the priest makes the sign of the cross five times; just after the memorial prayer he does the same. Preceding the first five crosses we find two offering prayers; following the second five crosses we find two offering prayers. Before the earlier offering prayers there are three mementos: of the Church, of the living, of the saints. After the later offering prayers there are three mementos: of the dead, of *us sinners,* of all nature. The first set of mementos is preceded by three signs of the cross, as the second set is followed by three signs

91

of the cross. The entire Canon is introduced by the Preface, ending in the hymn of angelic praise, the *Sanctus*. The entire Canon is concluded by the so-called Little Elevation, ending in a most solemn doxology.

The well-named Preface, the present introduction to the Canon, was originally the first prayer of the Canon, and it was an extended hymn after the fashion of the *Exsultet* still sung at the Easter Vigil. The dominant note of the Preface was, from the beginning, thanksgiving; the very word *eucharist* means, after all, *giving thanks*. One of the earliest Prefaces that we know thanks God for His blessings, beginning with creation and continuing through the provident guidance of God as shown in the leading events of the Old Testament. The hymn culminates, exactly as it does today, with the joyous and angelic triple *Sanctus: Holy, holy, holy, Lord God of hosts*.

The Preface of today still begins with the old acclamations — *Lift up your hearts,* and so on — still ends in the exultant *Sanctus,* is still a hymn of gratitude. It has, however, been sharply abbreviated, and the emphasis of thanks rests upon the particular feast or mystery that is being celebrated, for we now have 16 different Prefaces in the Roman missal. With two exceptions, the Prefaces have three parts: a declaration of general gratitude to God, particular thanks for the immediate reason or occasion, and a rich description of the angelic choirs, this last leading naturally to the *Sanctus*.

In the ordinary piety of our Mass assistance, the Preface may serve us in a double way. It can be our special moment of conscious, explicit gratitude to our good God for all the love and blessings He pours out upon us. And, of course, the Preface will alert us to even closer attention as the sublime climax of the sacred, sacrificial action approaches.

The last words before the Canon are a glad combination of the angelic *Holy, holy, holy* and the Palm Sunday *Hosanna* of our Lord's disciples and friends. In a new and even more significant context we say heartily once more, *Blessed is He who comes in the name of the Lord.* As the Advent liturgy has it in its own special context, *He will come and will not delay.* We stand ready, now, to give King Jesus reverent and joyous and loving welcome.

27. *Therefore, Father most kind, through Jesus Christ Your Son and our Lord we humbly ask and plead that You accept and bless these gifts, these offerings, this holy and spotless sacrifice* . . . (opening words of the Canon of the Mass).

Like most liturgical prayers, the initial words of what we may aptly call the crucial part of the Mass are addressed to God the Father. Said an early council of the Church: *Dirigatur oratio ad Patrem: Let prayer be directed to the Father.* Such procedure is strictly in accord with the promise and implicit instruction which our Savior Himself gave to His disciples at the Last Supper: *Whatever request you make of the Father in My name, I will grant . . . so that every request you make of the Father in My name may be granted you. . . . Believe Me, you have only to make any request of the Father in My name, and He will grant it to you.*

We in our private piety are liable to overlook that profound truth which is the theme of the Epistle to the Hebrews, a truth which Mother Church never forgets: that Christ our Lord and Savior is our High Priest, that is, the Mediator between us and God. We go to God *through* Christ, under the guidance of the Holy Spirit. Our Lord put the truth with extreme brevity and complete perfection when He said simply, *I am the way*.

Through our Mediator, then, the Church in the Mass now begs once more that God look kindly upon the gifts which are being offered to Him. Meanwhile the priest makes a triple sign of the cross over the bread and wine; the adjectives which are here applied to the offerings — *holy and spotless* — are, again, anticipatory.

At this solemn point a new element appears in the Mass liturgy. Up to now there have been prayers not a few, but, except for the passing reference in the Offertory to *all those present,* there have been no supplications for particular persons or intentions. Throughout the Canon, both before and after the Consecration, the petitions of the liturgy now become specific. Before all else, we pray in the Mass for the Church.

In every human grouping there must always exist a certain tension between the individual on the one hand and the group on the other. The situation is, of its nature, delicate. In any collectivity the vital importance of the individual must never be trampled under the collective foot or lost in the shuffling of a mob. Yet it must never be forgotten that the community is something more and something more significant than the sum of its members. Catholic piety will always possess a mild but legitimate individualistic character, if only because my most intimate and secret way of talking to God will not exactly be someone else's most personal way. Catholic theology would not dream of stepping between the veritable Holy Spirit and a particular soul.

Yet the far more menacing danger is that Catholic piety will be altogether too individualist and not sufficiently communal. It is simply imperative, it is urgent in the most literal way, that the Catholic understand that he lives and thinks and speaks and acts and prays and is saved, not in isolation, but as a member of the Church, as a living part of the Mystical Body of Christ. The Catholic must not only know *about* the Church, he must be *conscious* of the Church, he must consciously and explicitly act *with and within* the Church — in short, he must *love* the Church.

So in the Mass we pray first and fondly for the Bride of Christ, for our Holy Mother, for the Church herself. With reverence and filial affection we single out for special commendation to God our beloved Holy Father and our most reverend bishop. Then we include all those true because orthodox servants of Christ in the whole world — other bishops, all priests, religious brothers and sisters, all lay apostles — who are spending their lives in the interests of the Catholic and apostolic faith.

At the very outset of the Canon of the Mass the individual Catholic is lifted from his little place in a particular church, he is lifted out of all his petty selfhood, and placed in the shining ranks of a vast and splendid and holy host. Oh yes, God, please bless Your holy Catholic Church!

28. *Be mindful, Lord, of Your servants, men and women . . .* (the Memento of the Living, in the Canon of the Mass).

The first prayer of the most sacred part of the Mass is for the universal Church. The second prayer, more specific, is for particular members of the Church militant and is known as the Memento of the Living, in distinction from the remembrance of the departed which will follow later. At this point in the missal a space is left to remind the celebrant that now he may, as he pauses, name to God those living persons for

whom he particularly wishes to pray in this Mass. Here we
meet the first of the only two occasions on which the priest
is permitted to make any insertion into the strictly guarded
ritual of the Mass.

The Memento of the Living makes two categories of those
to be remembered: *Your servants, men and women,* and *all
those present.* In practice, the first grouping will subdivide
itself.

The priest at the altar and, presumably, all of the congregation who are closely following the Mass will first name the
living person, if such be the case, for whom he or each one
present is offering this Mass. Next, he will specifically mention others, such as his living parents, his brothers, his
sisters, to whom he is most closely and naturally bound.
Surely, also, he will explicitly remember the donor of the Mass.

It is a beautiful thing for any one of us to be called by
name in the holy sacrifice of the Mass. Those who are honestly
close to a priest may rejoice in the certainty that they are
often and perhaps daily named to God under the most exalted
circumstances.

Obviously, however, the celebrant of the Mass cannot delay
the sacrifice while he runs through a catalogue of names.
No doubt, therefore — and here, again, we may all follow
him — he will daily commend to God many, and indeed a
host of people, by means of ready categories: relatives, benefactors, friends, those for whom he is laboring, all who have
asked him to remember them. The religious priest will not
forget those who are truly his brothers *in Christ,* and it would
be a signal and wholesome exercise of Christian charity for
all of us resolutely to include in our prayer all the people
who are, in our lives, most difficult and disagreeable and
hostile and cantankerous. The exercise is both generous and

well-advised, for it may on some occasion generate a suspicion in the praying mind that cantankerousness is rarely all on one side.

Lastly the priest asks God to have a care for *all here present*. We may remark at once that here is one blessing that accrues any time we assist at Mass: we get ourselves prayed for.

The liturgy enters into a small but gracious discussion of *all here present*. It says that *their faith is known and their devotedness familiar* to God. It says both that the Mass is being offered for them and that they themselves *are offering this sacrifice of praise for themselves and for all their intentions*. It specifies the best of those intentions: *for the redemption of their souls, in hope of well-being and security*. The prayer ends by candidly reminding the *eternal God* that all these good people are praying hard to Him. There seems to be a mild, respectful hint that such good folk and good prayers deserve to be heard.

The whole liturgical passage is fine and admirable and consoling, but perhaps we might note particularly the explicit declaration that the laity, too, offer the Mass with the priest.

Again let us conceive the solidarity of the Christian community in the sublime sacrifice of the Mass. The Lord Christ is offering the Mass, but not Christ alone and in unapproachable isolation. The priest is offering the Mass, yet not the priest alone — is he not in essence a *mediator?* — nor even the priest in splendid conjunction with Christ the high priest. The Mass is being offered by Christ and the priest and the people. Does not the liturgy say of the faithful present: *who offer this sacrifice of praise?* And the Council of Trent has assured us that there are no mistakes in the Canon of the Mass.

29. *Being in fellowship with and reverently bringing to
mind, first, the ever glorious Virgin Mary, Mother of our
Lord Jesus Christ* . . . (the Commemoration of the Saints, in
the Canon of the Mass).

Thus far in the Canon of the Mass we have consciously put
ourselves in union with the whole Church militant. We have
prayed for the Church herself, for the Holy Father, for our
Bishop, for all who share our Catholic faith, for the living,
for all who are present at this Mass. Now, with a lyric leap, the
liturgy makes contact with the Church triumphant. Of course
we do not pray *for* the glorious ones whom we now recall.
We pray *to* them, or, more exactly, *through* them.

The initial words of this prayer merit attention: *Com-
municantes et memoriam venerantes, Communicating with
and venerating the memory of.* . . . The first participle contains that Catholic doctrine which we mention every time
we say the Creed — the Communion of Saints. Not by way of
metaphor but in sober theological and ontological reality we
on earth are actually *in fellowship with* the victorious crowned
in heaven as well as with the saved who, in purgatory, are
still undergoing their final purification. The second phrase of
the present liturgical passage prompts the liturgists to remark
the steady occurrence, in the Canon of the Mass, of words of
remembrance: *memoriam, memento, memory, remember,
mindful.* We cannot too often remind ourselves that the Mass
is a solemn reminder.

The concise catalogue of saints which we read here begins,
of course, with our Lady, the saint of saints, who, incidentally,
is mentioned five times in the Mass — supposing that the
Creed is said. There follow the names of the twelve Apostles,
Paul taking the place of Matthias, as might be expected in a

Roman liturgy. Next we meet the names of twelve martyrs: five popes, one bishop, the deacon Lawrence, and five laymen. John and Paul were brothers, and, for the consolation of the weary doctors in the congregation, Cosmas and Damian were physicians. Distaff saints will be mentioned later. However, the brief enumeration does end with the inclusive *and all Your saints.*

What do we ask of God through *the merits and prayers* of our Lady and these holy ones? *That in all things we may be fortified by the help of Your protection.* We are pleading, then, for strength and protection.

Even as the most sacred moment of the sacrifice approaches, Holy Mother Church does not prescind from practicalities, does not forget that her children are needy. The prayer suggests two of our most constant and pressing needs: strength for our weakness, protection against menacing dangers.

How many there are who come to Mass haunted by these very needs! So many in every congregation are sorely weakened by the heavy burdens they must carry from one day to the next. So many go in aching dread of the dangers, all too real, that lurk in the shadows of tomorrow. And is it not empirically true that somehow people go from Mass quieted and consoled and heartened and perhaps a little less afraid?

Let us consider, as we recite this Commemoration of the Saints, how powerful are the intercessors whom we invoke, how truly and tenderly they, who have been through it all, pity our labors and fears, how more than willing our good God is, seeing us about to offer Him His own beloved Son, to throw about us the strong, protecting fortification of His grace. As one looks again at that galaxy of saints one realizes, almost with a start, that they are *all* martyrs, beginning with the Queen of Martyrs and the Mother of Sorrows herself.

With every confidence we who are yet straining and struggling may call upon these who strained and struggled so heroically, even to the victorious end.

Surely God our Lord wishes us ever to take heart as we name and invoke His saints. They did it. So can we.

30. *So, then, Lord, we beg You, please, to accept this offering of our service and that of all Your family . . .* (the first offering prayer immediately before the Consecration in the Mass).

There is a sense in which the Memento of the Living and the Commemoration of the Saints constitute a kind of pause in the sacrificial action of the Mass. The liturgy now resumes the strictly sacrificial prayers. During the first of these prayers, of which there are just two before the Consecration, the priest spreads his hands, palms down and thumbs joined, over the offerings. What might be the significance of this unique gesture which does not otherwise occur in the Mass?

It was at one time thought that some connection existed between this imposition of hands in the Mass and the imposition of hands in the Old Testament ceremony of the scapegoat. That ancient ceremony was a ritual of expiation. The assembled people placed their hands on the goat in token of a transfer of guilt: the animal was symbolically laden with the sins of the people, and was then driven into the desert. But that religious rite was precisely *not* a sacrifice, because the goat was now technically impure, and so could not be offered to God.

The imposition of hands on the offerings in the Mass would seem rather to be a gesture of indication that this gift comes from this offerer, and from those whom he represents, and consequently signifies the identification of the offerer and the gift.

It cannot be too often insisted that unless the gift in sacrifice truly symbolizes the giver, the religious act of sacrifice is meaningless. God does not need man's gifts, and, in a sense, He does not desire them. What God desires and seeks and covets is man himself and man's honest love. In the Mass the people of God offer to their Father the supreme gift of His own divine Son, their Brother and Lord. But even that exalted offering must be, as it were, authentic. In the Mass we either offer ourselves to God in and with and through Christ, or we offer nothing.

Meanwhile, the prayer begs God our Lord graciously to accept the sacrifice, which is now designated as coming from God's *family*. So we read in the Epistle to the Romans: *All those who from the first were known to Him, He has destined from the first to be molded into the image of His Son, who is thus to become the eldest-born among many brethren.* Christ, the natural Son of God, is *the eldest-born* in God's *family*, and we, the adopted sons, are the *many brethren*. Touchingly, the Eldest becomes the victim for the sake of all, but willingly, but lovingly. Isaias said in prophetic vision: *A victim? Yet He Himself bows to the stroke.*

Now the prayer makes a threefold petition: that our lives may be lived in peace, that we may be saved from hell, that we may attain to everlasting happiness. One reflects immediately that this supplication leaves little to be desired.

The plea, *that You dispose our days in Your peace,* was added to the Mass in a troubled time; but not without the prompting of the Holy Spirit was the petition woven into the now unchanging part of the Mass. Sadly we must concede that *in this valley of tears* every time is a troubled time, and every age — indeed, every hour — must beg God to give peace to the world, peace to the Church, peace to the heart that is sore and fearful. *Dispose our days in Your peace:* Lord God, do, please do!

It may seem incongruous that just before the Consecration the liturgy makes mention of *eternal damnation.* Yet, why not? There is no gain in mincing words, and what is expressed here, first negatively and then positively, is one of the two final reasons why there is any Mass at all. Every Mass is offered for God's glory and man's salvation.

Certainly it is apt, on the threshold of the Consecration, to give a thought to heaven. As, at the sacred words, the Lord Christ comes down upon the altar, there is still nothing much for us to see with these bodily eyes of ours. But it will not always be so. We are pilgrims as yet, and in this time of wayfaring our only glimpse of Him whom we love is *sub his figuris, under these veils,* of bread and wine. Let us only be patient, let us do simply and honestly what in us lies, and at last the veils will fall away, the darkness will blaze with light, and we will see — *the eldest-born* of our *family.*

31. *God, we beg You, please, to make this offering in every way blessed, consecrated, approved, reasonable, and acceptable; that it may become for us the body and blood of Your dearly beloved Son, our Lord Jesus Christ* (the second prayer of offering before the Consecration in the Mass).

The final offering prayer before the Consecration in the Mass is notable in two ways: for its formal, heavy, legalistic language and for the first specific reference in the liturgy itself to the approaching Consecration.

In its nature this supplication does not differ from all the other entreaties in the Mass that God be pleased to accept the sacrifice. At first acquaintance one might feel surprised and even faintly irritated by that liturgical refrain of unworthiness, but presently we recall that here, in the unique religious act of sacrifice, we find the creature in direct dealing, on the highest level, with his Creator. In the relationship between man and God there is never room for smugness and complacency and self-assurance on the part of man, and the closer man approaches to God — as, par excellence, in the Mass — the less reason exists for breezy presumption. The Holy Sacrifice is, along with so much else, a surpassing exercise of the three theological virtues, but our hope, too, like our faith and our love, rests and centers upon Christ. Our Savior in His lifetime had certain sharp comments to make concerning *some who had confidence in themselves, thinking they had won acceptance with God. . . .*

The prayer asks that almighty God make and render our offerings thus and so — and the liturgy employs five separate adjectives to specify its request. We beg God to make our oblation *benedictam, adscriptam, ratam, rationabilem, acceptabilem.* The weighty, quasi-forensic terms seem to say: "Make our offering *blessed,* that is, sacred, no longer secular and profane; *recorded,* that is, officially and properly noted down and therefore set aside or dedicated, consecrated; *approved,* that is, ratified and so valid and legitimate; *reasonable,* or essentially fitting for rational man to offer to all-knowing God; *acceptable* to Your divine Majesty."

The reader is struck by the solemnity and deliberate formalism of the language here. It must not be that we draw near to the heart of the sacred mystery jocularly or casually or lightly.

And now at last we ask with a kind of wonderful simplicity that the earthy, material bread and wine *become for us the body and blood of . . . our Lord Jesus Christ.*

It is so fitting that at the moment before the Consecration the priest at the altar, in all his naked, human mortality and feebleness, appeal directly and, as it were, desperately, to the infinite power of God. I am a man. Who am I, that I should undertake to change one substance into another? What a supreme and mad alchemist I must be if, by any will or device of mine, I would fashion the living Christ out of coarse food and drink! But I am a priest. And therefore I will do this un-thinkable thing — but not without final appeal, before I utter the unutterable words, to the awful might and majesty of God. *God, we beg You, please,* turn this, upon the altar, into *the body and blood of Your dearly beloved Son, our Lord Jesus Christ.*

All is now ready. There is a stir in the soundless world of the supernatural, and around the altar, however humble, troops of invisible, pure spirits come to reverent attention. By a sure instinct the people in the church grow strangely quiet. The priest, who ought to be frozen in a kind of incredulous paralysis, quietly composes or rather numbs himself. We are ready for the coming of the Lord.

Be it so, then; come, Lord Jesus.

32. *. . . Who, on the day before He suffered, took bread into His holy and venerable hands, and raising His eyes to heaven, to You, God, His Father almighty, giving thanks to You, He blessed and broke it, and gave it to His disciples, saying: Take and eat. For this is My body* (Consecration of the bread in the Mass).

The last prayer before the Consecration of the Mass has ended in the glowing words: *Your most beloved Son, our Lord Jesus Christ.* Now, by means of the simple relative pronoun, a smooth transition is made from prayer to narrative. The narrative is that of the essential moment of the Last Supper, yet it is a composite account from various sources, and does not come verbatim from any of the Gospels. *Holy and venerable* hands is an addition of reverence, and the Lord's gesture of *raising His eyes to heaven* occurs in the gospel record of the miracle of the loaves and fish.

As the celebrant of the Mass pronounces these solemn but serene words, he performs, up to a point, the actions that are described: he takes the host between thumbs and forefingers, he raises his eyes, he makes the sign of the cross over the bread. He then bows low over the altar and, in a low tone, speaks the efficacious words that achieve and realize the sublime sacrifice.

Nothing is so calculated to humble a priest and make him deeply thoughtful (and priestly) as the realization that at the climactic moment of the Mass, and hence of the priest's daily life, he does not speak in his own person, but in the Person of Christ. Up to those final words the narrative has flowed in the grammatical third person, but at the last the priest does not say: "This is Christ's body." No, but: *This is My Body.* Once in each day, with terrifying literalness, the priest becomes Christ.

So the Lord Christ comes down upon the altar. There are various truths to be remembered in connection with this coming.

In the Mass Christ comes among us in His humanity. Our Lord's epiphany here is not at all like the visit of a bright angel, nor is it after the manner of a vision or most profound supernatural illumination. Christ is upon the altar as He was present in His lifetime on earth, as He sat at table with friends or enemies, as He conversed with His disciples, as He stroked the heads of happy children. That is, our Lord is physically, corporally, and (though in a special mode) spatially present.

However, Christ is corporally present in the Mass in a humanity which is now glorified. Despite industrious speculation, we know precious little about the state or condition of the glorified body, and all that we do know or suspect seems uncommonly contradictory, as that the glorified body is palpable yet incorruptible, that it can eat, yet need not. It is enough, though, to grasp that the glorified body is strictly impassible — no longer susceptible to pain or suffering of any sort. So, then, the coming of Christ in the Mass is absolutely triumphant. He comes not as Christ suffering but as Christ who has suffered, and who overcame His suffering. The epiphany of our Lord on the altar, despite all its humble seeming, is the showing forth of the conquering King.

There is another characteristic of the advent of the Lord Christ in the Mass, but this must be reserved for further discussion. It is by no means unreasonable, nor should it cause bewilderment, to remind our devoted Catholic people that they must distinguish between the Eucharist and the Mass; that is, between the Eucharist as a sacrament and the Eucharist as a sacrifice. The special point to be noted is that the coming of Christ in the sacrifice is *transient*. In the Mass the Lord comes, and He goes. The tabernacle, for all that it rightly and richly means to us, must not be allowed to obscure the brief but tremendous action that takes place on the altar itself. To this deep truth we will return. Only let us observe the particular preciousness, in this transient life, of all that is beautiful, sublime — and transient.

33. *In like manner, after He had supped, taking also this excellent chalice into His holy and venerable hands, and giving thanks to You, He blessed and gave it to His disciples, saying: Take and drink of this, all of you, for this is the chalice of My blood . . .* (Consecration of the wine in the Mass).

Anyone who has ever attended, with any sensitivity, a Roman Catholic Mass will surely attest that the most impressive moment occurs when, after each Consecration, the priest raises above his head for all to see, first the host, then the chalice. It is perfectly evident at every Mass that there exists at this point a clear and solid understanding on the part of the congregation as to precisely what is taking place. We need not now concern ourselves that the elevation is not of the most ancient origin or that it is not found explicitly in the Oriental rites. We do have the elevation, and, best of all, our people grasp it and love it.

Indeed, the devoted Catholic laity so appreciate the showing forth of our Lord in His sacramental garb that a certain mild caution or suggestion may here not be out of place. The related ideas of adoration and sacrifice are anything but exclusive of one another, but they are not identical, either. Sacrifice is at once included in adoration, since it is one of the specific acts by which adoration is expressed, and goes beyond adoration, because it likewise involves and conveys thanksgiving, expiation, and petition. Our adoration of Christ present in the Mass is significantly distinct from our adoration of Christ present in the tabernacle. The formed and informed Catholic will understand that in the Mass the Lord Christ comes not (if we may riskily put it so) in order to *be,* but in order to *do.* Our Savior becomes corporally present in the Mass not for the sake of being among us, but for the exalted and sacred purpose of repeating mystically the sacrificial immolation He physically made of Himself on Calvary. In short, the Consecration and Elevation should emphasize and not obscure the central truth that the Mass is a sacrifice.

This is the theological reason why the *transience* of Christ in the Mass — His coming, His immolation, His going — is profoundly meaningful and should be appreciatively noted.

When He came near Jericho, there was a blind man sitting there by the wayside begging. And he, hearing a multitude passing by, asked what it meant; so they told him, that Jesus of Nazareth was going past. Whereupon he cried out: Jesus, son of David, have pity on me.

There is undeniable pathos in this truth of the passage of the Lord in the Mass. But the truth must not be left thus incomplete. Let us advert now to an expression that occurs in the Consecration of the wine: *For this is the chalice of My blood, of the new and eternal testament.*

Now the biblical word *testament,* starting with the primary significance of a legal instrument, comes at once to mean *covenant* or *convention* or *pact* or *agreement.* The Old Testament is the history of God's original covenant or pact with a chosen people. But the blood of Christ is the efficacious sign *of the new and eternal testament* — that later and more holy and final pact and agreement between faithful God and believing man.

What are the broad terms of this new pact? On man's side, faith and love and obedience. On God's side, the promise of grace now and salvation forever.

A conclusion follows which is not to be missed. The coming of Christ in the Mass is brief, and is followed by His going. The presence of Christ in the Mass is strictly transient. Yet that coming, that short presence, that passing by of

Christ is a sacred pledge and promise. *Pignus vitae aeternae,* sings the Church of the Eucharist; it is a *pledge of eternal life.*

And though I do go away, to prepare you a home, I am coming back; and then I will take you to Myself, so that you too may be where I am.

34. *As often as you do this, in memory of Me will you do it* (the words in the Mass which immediately follow the Consecration).

Before and after the elevation of each now sacred species, the priest at the altar genuflects in external manifestation of interior adoration. As he makes the last genuflection, he says in a low tone, still firmly speaking in the person of Christ: *As often as you do this, in memory of Me will you do it.*

So is emphasized, at the most solemn moment of the sacrifice, the truth that is more than implied throughout the Canon, that the Mass, together with all else that it most certainly is, is a memorial, an unfailing reminder of the Lord Christ. This is the point of major stress that St. Paul recounts, in his First Epistle to the Corinthians, when he speaks about the institution of the Eucharist. Three times in three successive verses Paul says — echoing St. Luke — that the Eucharist Sacrifice is a memorial of Christ.

What, exactly or at least especially, are we to remember about Christ at the gentle, steady prompting of the Mass? St. Paul tells us: *So it is the Lord's death that you are heralding* (proclaiming, that is) *until He comes.*

The longer one ponders the Christian revelation, the more clearly one begins to understand why the cross is the first ornament, the first symbol, the first and last lesson of this religion. From the existence of God the Creator to the fact of immortality, every article in the Christian Creed is important, but the central belief of all is expressed in the words: *who . . . suffered under Pontius Pilate, was crucified, died and was buried.* One notes the odd explicitness of *and was buried.* The inclination would be to murmur: "But of course. Need we insist on *that?*" Yet, there are the painfully explicit words, forever graven in the Creed. Indeed, Christ did truly die, and in torment, and for us.

Of course, the death of our Lord is never separated in Christian belief, exactly as it is never separated in the inspired writings of St. Paul, from the resurrection of our Lord. Sometimes we see a crucifix in which Christ is portrayed not in agony but serene and majestic and triumphant. The artistic intuition in that instance is soundly theological.

Whenever the essentially unchanging Mass is celebrated through the changing liturgical year, we are simultaneously reminded of the death of our Lord; but as we pass gladly from feast to fast to festival again, we are reminded of all the other substantial truths about Him. Wisely led by Holy Mother Church, we annually commemorate our Savior's coming among us, His infancy, the major events of His public life, His achieving of redemption, His ascension, His continued presence in the Eucharist, His Sacred Heart, and so on. Thus, on the last Sunday in October, we call to mind and commemorate in the Mass not only the death of Christ, but His kingship.

Anyone who wishes may say that kings are out of date, but that is exactly like saying that clothes are out of date because, men (for the most part) now no longer wear robes but — in the Chestertonian expression — a trouser on either leg. The king is the leader, and the leader, despite the appalling antics of the Khrushchevs and Castros of this long-suffering world, will never be outmoded. Men simply must have someone to whose cause they willingly rally, whose authority they recognize, whose policy they accept, whom they openly and avowedly follow, whom, indeed, they esteem and actually love.

It is this human need and the providential answer to it that we celebrate in the Mass and liturgy of this day. We Christian men ought to glory beyond measure in *our* King and Leader. He is the only one who never disappoints, from whom no antics need be feared, who is indeed worth loving, who absolutely guarantees final victory. Hail, Christ the King!

35. *Wherefore, Lord, we Your servants and likewise Your holy people, calling to mind the blessed Passion of the same Christ, Your Son, our Lord, together with His Resurrection from the grave, and also His glorious Ascension into heaven* . . . (prayer of Remembrance immediately after the Consecration in the Mass).

It might reasonably be expected that the first liturgical words after the climactic moment of the Mass would constitute a pronouncement of singular depth and significance. Such a pronouncement we do indeed find. In addition, we are assured by the liturgists that "this prayer is one of the oldest parts of the liturgy . . . a prayer of the greatest antiquity, which most probably goes back to apostolic times."

This measured address, during which the priest again makes the sign of the cross five times, recapitulates the triple significance of the Mass. The Mass is a memorial; it is a sacrifice; it is a sacred meal.

We have already examined the memorial aspect of the Mass. We observe now that the liturgy here recalls our Lord's *blessed Passion . . . Resurrection . . . glorious Ascension.* Now look back to the prayer which is said at the center of the altar after the completion of the Offertory: *Accept, holy Trinity, this offering which we make to You in memory of the Passion, Resurrection and Ascension of Jesus Christ our Lord.* Such emphasis cannot be either accidental or incidental. Over and over it must be said that what we commemorate in every Mass is the death of Christ, but that death cannot and must not be separated from the triumph that follows in our Savior's return from the grave and His exaltation, as coequal, at the side of His Father.

Next, the Mass in its deepest essence is nothing other or less than the highest religious act of which man is capable, the act of sacrifice. So this prayer repeats in new form what has already been said more than once: *We, Your servants* [the clergy] *and likewise Your holy people* [the laity] *. . . offer to Your excellent Majesty . . . a pure Victim, a holy Victim, an immaculate Victim. . . .* We cannot miss the insistence on the innocence of the One who is offered in vicarious expiation for our sorry, undeniable guilt.

We now encounter the first explicit reference in the ritual to the final aspect of the Mass. That which we offer to God is not only a *Victim:* it is also *the holy bread of eternal life and the chalice of everlasting salvation.* Here is the first liturgical intimation that in the Mass not only do we give Christ to His Father as our gift, but also the Father will give Him back to us as our food. This is the earliest hint that the sacrifice will end in a banquet.

That which all religion undertakes finally to accomplish is the union of God and man. Any religious system which does not sight this objective and strive for it is not a religion at all. At best it is no more than ethics or humanitarianism, and at worst it is no more than myth. But could the noblest religious instinct devise or imagine an instrument more perfectly calculated to bring about such union than the Mass? Because the Mass is a living memorial of the death and victory of Christ, it brings God in Christ powerfully, steadily, into the human mind. Because the Mass is a sacrifice, and especially a sacrifice of expiation, it makes peace between God and man through Christ the Victim. *Yes, God was in Christ,* cries St. Paul, *reconciling the world to Himself, establishing in our hearts His message of reconciliation, instead of holding men to account for their sins.* Because the Mass culminates in the sacred meal wherein Christ Himself is the food, there ensues the most intimate conceivable union between man and God in the Person of our Lord: *He who eats My flesh, and drinks My blood, lives continually in Me, and I in him.*

36. *Upon these gifts be pleased to look with a kindly and serene countenance and to accept them, as You were graciously pleased to accept the gifts of Your just servant Abel and the sacrifice of our patriarch Abraham and that which Your high priest Melchisedech offered You, a holy sacrifice, a spotless victim* (prayer of the Three Types, after the Consecration in the Mass).

In this ancient and provocative prayer of the Canon the emphasis on the Mass as a sacrifice is renewed. First we encounter the familiar refrain, that almighty God may be *graciously pleased to accept* the offering we make to Him. No sacrifice is complete when it is offered; it must be ac-

cepted. Next, the liturgy appeals to the example of three Old
Testament sacrifices which God did accept. All these events
and persons are mentioned in the first book of the Bible, the
Book of Genesis.

In the fourth chapter of Genesis we read: *Abel, too, brought
an offering, and his offering was out of the firstborn of his
flock, with their fat. On Abel, and on his offering, the Lord
looked with favor.* The *just Abel,* as our Savior Himself calls
him, has always been regarded as a figure of our Lord, for as
Abel the innocent was slain by his wicked brother, so the
sinless Christ was slain by His sinful brothers in humanity.
Moreover, the example of Adam's second son is particularly
apt in the present liturgical context, for Genesis sharply contrasts the offering of Abel, which God accepted, with that of
Cain, which God rejected.

The second type or figure is *our patriarch Abraham.* The
liturgy of the Church — and herein we may allow ourselves
to be instructed by our wise Mother — never forgets the
strong link between the Old Law and the New, between the
venerable synagogue and the ever-young Bride of Christ, between the true Jew and the true Catholic. The immediate
reference here is to chapter 22 of Genesis, where we read the
chilling and mysterious story of the command to Abraham
to sacrifice his *beloved son Isaac.* The point is, of course, the
absolute obedience, pliability, and dependence of Abraham
before almighty God.

Lastly, we encounter in this cosmic, mystical prayer the
shadowy yet majestic figure of that Melchisedech who looms so
prominent in Scripture. In Genesis, chapter 14, we learn of
the return of Abraham after a victorious expedition against a
quartet of hostile, raiding chieftains: *And as he came back,*

the king of Sodom went out to meet him . . . Melchisedech, too, was there, the king of Salem. And he, priest as he was of the most high God, brought out bread and wine with him, and gave him this benediction: On Abraham be the blessing of the most high God, maker of heaven and earth.

Amazingly, since he had nothing to do with the Levitical, Jewish priesthood, this magnificent personage was revered in Hebrew thought. Psalm 109 mentions him — *Thou art a priest forever, according to the order of Melchisedech* — and that Psalm, which is manifestly messianic, is quoted by Christ Himself. Above all, Melchisedech stands at the very center of the Epistle to the Hebrews, the inspired letter which eloquently expounds the priesthood of Christ.

It is easy to see the aptness, as a type of our Lord, of this primeval priest-king of Jerusalem (Salem) who, contrary to scriptural practice, is introduced in Genesis abruptly, without human genealogy. But, of course, the most telling point of all, and what makes the portentous name come perfectly in the Mass, is that Melchisedech, in an age of bloody sacrifices, offered sacrifice to God in *bread and wine.*

Perhaps the most fitting reaction to this liturgical prayer is to be genuinely impressed with it. Ancient and majestic men and deeds move gravely through the sacred pageantry of the Mass. The curtains of the most distant past draw apart, and giant, holy figures come forward — for what purpose? To take their respectful, reverent stand upon the timeless Calvary of the Mass. For all these figures of antiquity, with all their splendor and holiness, are figures indeed. They shrink, they pale, they become shadows as they gather round the priceless Victim and supreme priest-king, the Lord Christ.

37. *Humbly we beg You, almighty God, to command that these gifts be carried by the hands of Your holy angel to Your altar on high, in the sight of Your divine majesty* . . . (the last of the Offering Prayers in the Canon of the Mass).

Still the Church prays in the Mass for divine ratification of the sacrifice. The language of the liturgy now brightens with an imagery that is at once reminiscent of the Old Testament angelology and strongly reflective of the Apocalypse of St. John.

In the Book of Tobias the archangel Raphael, that celestial physician and psychiatrist, declares: *When thou, Tobias, wert praying, and with tears . . . I, all the while, was offering that prayer of thine to the Lord.* St. John, in his flaming vision, speaks several times of *the golden altar* which stands in the presence of God, and at one point he writes: *There was another angel that came and took his stand at the altar, with a censer of gold; and incense was given him in plenty, so that he could make an offering on the golden altar before the throne, out of the prayers said by all the saints.*

In such rich scriptural terms the Church begs that the sacred sacrifice which is offered on earth may be approved, ratified, and accepted in heaven, that the oblation which is made *at this altar* — and here the priest reverently kisses the altar table — may be angelically borne to God's *altar on high.* The liturgy does not specify a particular bright spirit for this splendid task, and a very old text of the Canon mentions heavenly ministers in the plural, but perhaps we may imagine a suggestion here of St. Michael, the guardian of the Church.

Now we meet the second explicit reference in the sacrifice to the sacred culmination that is yet to come: *that as many of us as, at this altar, shall partake and receive the holy body and blood of Your Son, may be filled with every heavenly blessing and grace.*

When we examine the liturgy of the Mass it becomes amazing that Jansenism and Jansenistic trends should ever have succeeded, as they most certainly did, in keeping perfectly good people from receiving Holy Communion. The liturgy leaves no doubt that the sacred eating is the normal, natural consequence and conclusion of the sacrificial act. One would think that any perceptive Catholic, reading this prayer at a Mass in which he does not intend to receive Holy Communion, would experience at least a vague, if not a painful, sense of being somehow left out of the completeness of the sacred action. We give Christ to God in the Mass. At once God looks to give Christ back to us in Holy Communion.

(Let us studiously avoid any comment on those good but unaware people who unnecessarily or lightly or mechanically receive Holy Communion *before* Mass.)

Aptly we ask for *every heavenly blessing and grace,* for this noble prayer is all *heavenly.* As in the case of the sacraments, the entire liturgy and the whole economy of the Church, one of the long-range effects of the Mass is gradually to detach our human affections from all that is strictly material and secular and earthy, and fix them on what is spiritual and eternal and supernatural, in short, on what is *heavenly.* The project is a formidable one and, as might be expected, doesn't always work out to perfection. Still, the perceptive Catholic whom we mentioned will understand what way the wind that is the Holy Spirit is blowing. We all of us must periodically remind ourselves that things won't always be this way, whatever way they are; that as far as this life, with all its joys and sorrows and tedium, is concerned, all we have to do is wait, and there'll be some big changes made.

38. *Be mindful also, Lord, of Your servants, men and women . . . who are gone before us with the sign of faith, and sleep in the sleep of peace* (Memento of the Dead in the Mass).

In the Canon of the Mass there are three remembrance prayers before the Consecration, and one of these is the Memento of the Living. Similarly, there are three remembrance prayers after the Consecration, and one of these is the Memento of the Dead. During the most sacred interval of the sacrifice, Holy Mother Church remembers and commends to God not only her laboring children in the land of the living, but, with the same maternal tenderness, all those sons and daughters *who are gone before us with the sign of faith* (baptism), *and sleep in the sleep of peace.*

It is both instructive and consoling to note how the Church describes the situation of those who have died and are now in purgatory — for if they are not in purgatory, there is no point in praying for them. First, Mother Church uses for harsh death the gentle word *sleep,* and she at once adds that this is a *sleep of peace.* No doubt the Church is thinking, as did the prince of English poets, of the blessed calm that shows even on the features after the struggles and squirmings and heartaches and headaches of this mortal existence: "After life's fitful fever, he sleeps well." But shall we read no more than blank surcease and cessation in those lovely words, *the sleep of peace?* Surely, much more. Perhaps we do not commonly think of the souls in purgatory as being at peace. But they are, really. They are suffering, indeed, but they are absolutely and finally saved, as you and I, kind reader, are not — yet.

It warms the heart to reflect how the Catholic Church

every day and Catholics as often as they go to Mass explicitly remember their beloved dead. Without tinge of malice or complacency, but only with grateful gladness, we may wonder how many people or institutions other than the Church let no day pass without calling to mind their dear departed. And what a comfort it is to realize that each one of us, when we have passed from this mortal scene — "no longer in the picture," as the insurance salesman says gently — will be remembered in daily Mass until we have in fact and in truth and in deed arrived at the deepest and most durable peace of all.

For this remembrance, we must understand, is something far more substantial than fond and faithful recollection; it is a thing immeasurably superior to a flower or a tear. This memento is efficacious. We do not merely recall our dead, we pray for them; and we pray for them with all the power of liturgical prayer in the course of the highest act of religion, the act of sacrifice, and in union with the definitive and infinitely perfect sacrifice. It is good to commend our departed to God in any prayer. It is best to do so in the Mass.

The memento ends with a description of heaven. Heaven is a *place of refreshment, light, and peace.*

There is no need or use for mournful pessimism, but it is difficult to deny that for everyone periodically, and for not a few as a matter of almost daily fact, life on earth can be a time of weariness, darkness, and trouble. For any number of Catholics, the half-hour they spend at Mass is the least exhausting period in the day or the week. So many people are groping their way through life as through a thick fog, never seeing their way far ahead, rarely knowing where to turn or what to do next. And, in some cases, troubles and shocks and difficulties seem to come in battalions. Yet re-

member: all this, for the brave and faithful ones who battle
through, will be succeeded, on the solemn word of the Bride
of Christ, by everlastingly welcome *refreshment, light, and
peace.*

As the years of our lives pass and as our Masses blessedly
multiply, we begin to notice a touching thing. One by one,
more and more of the names which are dear to us pass from
one side of the Consecration to the other. When we are young,
we must perforce abbreviate the list of the living whom we
love and for whom we would pray. But the day comes when
we must start to abbreviate the remembrance of those whom
we loved once and love still, but *who are gone before us.*
They have changed their place in the liturgy, but they are
with us yet where being together is the most meaningful
togetherness in this world: in the Mass.

39. *To us sinners also, Your servants, who hope in the abun-
dance of Your mercies, please grant some part and fellowship
with Your holy apostles and martyrs: with John, Stephen,
Matthias* . . . (the prayer, in the Canon, for ourselves).

The petition which, at this point, the priest and the people
at Mass make for themselves is yet another plea for eternal
happiness, the theme occurring both at the start and at the
end of the prayer. Moreover, the present supplication is
marked by a particular sense of lowliness and unworthiness.
We speak of ourselves simply and flatly as *sinners,* although
earlier the congregation was commended to almighty God as
Your holy people. (Both descriptions are just.) We modestly
ask only for *some part and fellowship* with the saints, who
have loved and served God so nobly and who have attained

glory beyond all telling. We beg to be admitted into that splendid company, not, however, on any grounds of *our merit*, but solely through God's *free pardon*.

Again we recognize the Church's insistence on the only fitting attitude for the creature as he comes face to face with his Creator in the exalted religious transaction that is sacrifice.

There is an unmistakable parallelism, but without any repetition, between the list of saints here and the similar catalogue before the Consecration. In that earlier commemoration our Lady was mentioned first and separately, and then we read the names of the twelve Apostles (Paul taking the place of Matthias and being mentioned immediately after Peter) and twelve martyrs. In the present prayer John the Baptist, who is far more consequential in the Gospels, in the liturgy and in heaven than contemporary piety would suggest, occupies the special lead position. He is followed by seven male apostle-martyrs and seven martyrs of the gentler but no less hardy sex. St. Matthias now receives his due, finding honored place between the protomartyr Stephen and Paul's stalwart companion and occasional antagonist, Barnabas. The appealing feminine names are those of two North African martyrs (if the tradition be sound), two maidens of Sicily, and three specially beloved Roman martyrs, the very young Agnes, Cecilia the songbird, and the widow Anastasia.

Into this excellent company, which is rounded out by the usual concluding expression, *and with all Your saints,* we ask to be admitted; with these we beg *some part and fellowship.* The hope and prospect is a thrilling one.

Since we know ourselves to be *sinners,* there can be no question of making our own way into such spiritually sparkling society. For happiness such as this we pray, simply. In the Latin of this passage there is an attractive antithesis.

We petition God our Lord to be toward us *not the weigher of merit, but the granter of pardon.* The English may not be elegant, but the bold contrast is worth noting. God's justice and mercy are juxtaposed, and we take refuge in the one, since we dare not appeal to the other.

Nobis quoque peccatoribus, To us sinners also, are among the few words which the celebrant, according to the rubrics, says aloud in the Canon of the Mass. It may be considered that during this most holy part of the sacrificial action the priest withdraws, in a sense, into a certain intimacy with the Divine Majesty. As in the olden time, the chosen representative of the people, he who is the appointed mediator between them and their God, ascends the holy mountain and, lost in a cloud of unknowing, stands alone — but always for the people, always with God. On this rare occasion when he speaks from the cloud, the priest shows that he has not forgotten who or what he is: *To us sinners.* . . .

It is frightening for a priest to do what he should, to think and write about the Mass. He begins to glimpse the state and task and holiness to which he is called.

Envy, if you will, the priest in that cloud with God. But pray for him. He is a sinner, too.

40. *Through Him* (Christ), *Lord, You create, sanctify, vivify, bless, and give to us all these ever-good things* (the blessing of all things, toward the close of the Canon of the Mass).

As every Catholic senses, the Mass is and will remain, on the deepest level, a mystery. The ritual of the Mass, though, will commonly yield its secrets to reverent examination. The only portion of the ceremonial which may continue to mystify even the most attentive Catholic is the prayer and action which we now encounter. Making the sign of the cross three times over the consecrated elements, the priest whispers the measured words which make our present text. What is the meaning of this puzzling ceremony?

We must first recall a procedure in ancient liturgy which, like the offertory procession with which it was connected, has been lost in the passage of time.

We know, of course, that at the Offertory of the primitive Mass the people came themselves to the altar with their own gifts of bread and wine. But bread and wine were not the only offerings. People are ingenious as well as generous, and they will always and rightly prefer to give what they do have rather than not give what they don't have. So the faithful of an earlier and simpler time, in the dear days before instant-anything, brought happily to the altar and to God a wide range of gifts. They gave wax and oil and milk and grapes and honey and wool and flour and probably had to be restrained from bringing cats and dogs and pet birds.

The instinct at work was completely sound. All things are created by God, all things belong to God, all things may and really should be given back to God. Besides, religious men have always sensed that when an object has been presented to God and has been properly and ritually blessed, it becomes a different, more significant, and much more valuable thing. In the light of unchanging human nature, we hesitantly wonder whether some of the faithful in days gone by did not include in their offerings items which they hoped to get back — for, following the Mass, the nonconsecrated gifts were distributed to the poor — *after* they had been blessed.

However that may be, this ceremony which remains imbedded in the Mass liturgy is the remnant of the blessing of all the gifts that had been offered. Mother Church, in her wisdom and holiness, does bless everything. Good people, in their piety, want everything to be blessed. And both Church and faithful knew from the beginning that any blessing which was closely connected with the Mass and the Eucharist would be the richest blessing of all.

The faithful at Mass today may understand the blessing of all things in the widest sense, as precisely the blessing of *all* things: themselves, their homes, their possessions, their jobs, their food, and, indeed, the whole wide world of God's creation. There are two ways of looking at everything: the way of secular man and the way of religious man. Secular man looks at the vast universe and sees mystery indeed, but only the mystery of *things*. He wonders what that vagrant molecule or neutron is up to, and how two galaxies happened to get into a dilly of a smashup many millions of years ago. Religious man looks at the universe and sees mystery that is at once deeper and clearer, the mystery that lies *beneath* things. He wonders at the infinite majesty of the Creator who must be responsible for all this, and he marvels at the secret truth which is not so secret, after all. He begins to know that God creates because God loves. And then that man will feel strongly inclined and indeed obliged to love back.

Nobody knows, as yet, whether rational animals bide on any of those worlds which are daily, for weal or woe, wheeling about us. If there are such, we have no idea what destiny and plan God their Creator has for them. We feel entirely cordial toward all possible Martians, however. Every day, in our Mass, we bless *all* of God's creation.

41. *Through Him, and with Him, and in Him, is to You, God the Father almighty, in the unity of the Holy Spirit, all* *honor and glory, forever and ever. Amen* (the conclusion of the Canon of the Mass).

Beginning with what we now call the Preface, the Canon of the Mass is a single, sublime prayer which accompanies and expresses the essential sacrificial act. Now, as the Canon draws to a close, the liturgy prescribes a ritual action of particular antiquity and a verbal formula of special solemnity.

The action is known as the Little Elevation. Taking the consecrated Host between thumb and forefinger of his right hand, the priest five times makes the sign of the cross with the Host: thrice over the uncovered chalice, twice between himself and the chalice. Then, holding the Host over the mouth of the cup, with his left hand he lifts the chalice slightly from the square of linen (corporal) on which it stands.

Unobtrusive as this ceremony is, we have here the remnant of the one Elevation in the earliest Mass ritual. What is now our Elevation was introduced only in the Middle Ages. It must be admitted that when the Canon is regarded properly as a single, prolonged, Eucharistic prayer, the showing of the sacred species to the people comes aptly at the end of that prayer and immediately before the Eucharistic banquet. Since, in modern usage, the priest says Mass facing away from the congregation, this Little Elevation will inevitably be obscured, and the laity must be alert if they are not to miss a significant action.

The words which accompany the Little Elevation are solemn. They constitute the majestic doxology or formula of praise which is the ritual conclusion of the Canon of the Mass: *Per Ipsum et cum Ipso et in Ipso.* The first preposition expresses the mediation of Christ our Redeemer and everlasting High Priest; the second declares our union with Him; the third, introducing a favorite Pauline phrase, suggests the doctrinal reality that is the Mystical Body.

The layman at Mass may not be able to see the Little Elevation, but as he reads in his missal these measured words, he may take them to heart and plant them in his mind as the epitome of his whole Christian life. The man who professes belief in and claims to follow the program of Christ is called upon to live *through Him and with Him and in Him.*

No one should grow either disheartened or cynical because there are any number of Christian men who are unimpressed with this lofty religious formula, just as they are uninspired by any high religious ideal. We need only recall our Savior's realistic comments on the many who are called and the few who are chosen, His somewhat grim parables of the tares in the wheat field and the mixed and mixed-up catch of fish. All this must not dim our realization that a vast and devoted army of men and women who believe in Christ do most genuinely and in the most practical manner wish to live *through Him and with Him and in Him.* Both religiously and otherwise, good and brave people do not wear their hearts on their sleeves.

The major doxology that we know is, of course, the Gloria in the Mass, as the most familiar doxology is our "Glory be to the Father." Here, at the Little Elevation, is the splendid doxology which forms the peroration of the Canon of the Mass. The complete Trinitarian formula is present, and we reverently pray that to the Three Persons who are one God may be rendered *all honor and glory, forever and ever.*

Ideally, the *Amen* at the end of the Canon ought to be pronounced by all the people. In one of our earliest sources for the Mass liturgy we read that at the end of what we now call the Canon "the people give their consent by saying:

'Amen.' " Perhaps someday this admirable custom and cry of holy faith and unity will be restored. Meanwhile, let all in their hearts, as the sacred, sacrificial act, the renewal of Calvary, ends, "give their consent by saying: *'Amen.'* "

IV. THE COMMUNION

42. *Let us pray. Taught by our Savior's command and following His divine instruction we make bold to say: Our Father, who art in heaven . . .* (introduction to the Pater Noster in the Mass).

We enter now upon the fourth and final portion of the Mass. First there was the Fore-Mass, those readings and prayers which end with the Gospel or, when it is recited, the Creed. Next came the Offertory, the preparation of the sacrifice and the initiation of the true sacrificial action. There follows the Canon of the Mass, the center and heart of the sacred re-enactment. The last section of the Mass is the Communion, the sacrificial meal.

From the strictly historical point of view, sacrifice and sacrificial eating have been so regularly associated that one wonders if they are not somehow religiously inseparable. At any rate, the sixth chapter of St. John's Gospel, together with the simple human fact that Christ our Lord instituted His mystical sacrifice under the form of bread and wine, leaves no possible doubt that our Savior intended the Eucharistic Sacrifice to end in a Eucharistic meal. St. Paul makes it certain beyond challenge that such was the clear, factual understanding of the apostolic Church.

It is so very striking that of all the ways in which the Church might have ritually approached the Communion which climaxes the Mass, she chose to do so by the simple recitation of the Our Father. Holy Mother Church, ever guided by the Holy Spirit, is most disarming and seemingly ingenuous when she is most wise. Let us unhesitatingly be taught by this heavenly wisdom. The best way to prepare for Holy Communion is to say with meaning the Our Father.

In the brief, eloquent exordium which precedes the prayer, the liturgy directs our attention to two aspects of the Our Father: its unique, exalted origin, and the daring of it.

As everyone knows, the Our Father is the only prayer which we have, by way of instruction, from the lips of Christ Himself. We do read, in the four Gospels, other prayers which our Lord made, and we do well to repeat, in our own needs, those same addresses to God: *My Father, if this chalice may not pass me by, but I must drink it, then Thy will be done;* and *Father, into Thy hands I commend My spirit.* Yet the Our Father remains the only prayer which God's Son directly told us to say.

The daring that is noted here resides in the familiar, intimate address by which the creature speaks to his Creator. We Christians are so completely accustomed to thinking of God as a father that we can hardly believe that men generally did not always think thus. We forget that the fatherhood of God, in the special, not at all metaphorical sense that by baptism we are actually sons by divine adoption, is one of the insistences of the Christian revelation. It is attractive that a creature should by metaphor or even in created dependence and hence religious courtesy address his Creator as *Father.* It is stunning that the creature should in fact and reality call God *Father* because he is truly God's adopted son.

It has been said so often that the Our Father is the perfect model of petitionary prayer. Of the seven petitions that our Lord taught us — seven, like three and forty, is one of the holy numbers — the last four pertain to our own needs, and, essentially, they leave nothing to be desired. Good people wonder much about petitionary prayer. They wonder not only whether or not this or that request will be granted, but even whether or not they should make it. There is one firm and absolute answer that can be offered to all who are uncertain how to talk to God by way of supplication. They should say the Our Father.

Since the Lord's Prayer occurs where it does in the Mass, we will inevitably, at Mass, attend particularly to the plea, *Give us this day our daily bread.* It is not necessary to confine this petition to the Eucharistic bread which we are about to receive in Holy Communion. On the other hand, it is well to think about, and ask for, first things first.

43. *Deliver us, we implore You, Lord, from all evils, past, present, and to come, and by the intercession of the blessed and glorious Mary ever virgin, Mother of God . . .* (codicil to the Our Father in the Mass).

The final petition of the Our Father, *But deliver us from evil,* is voiced in the Mass by the acolytes or sung by the choir in the form of a rejoinder to the celebrant's recitation of the body of the beloved prayer. In a whisper the priest adds: *Amen.* At once he appends a supplication which is clearly an enlargement of that closing plea in the Our Father. It is sometimes called the "prayer for deliverance."

We ask first, in sweeping terms, to be set free *from all evils, past, present, and to come.*

At this point there is no hint as to the nature of those *evils* from which we seek deliverance, but we beg to be clear of *all* of them, and the familiar chronological classification is added to enforce universality. The Church's maternal concern for *all* the concerns of her children is evident, but as we intently repeat this prayer at Mass we may save ourselves from illusion by reflecting reasonably on certain distinctions in the complex matter of evil. There is evil which is only too real, and evil which is more apparent than real. There is that which is totally evil, and that which is but partly or even briefly evil. There is evil which is escapable, and evil which is finally inevitable.

Holy Mother Church has no prayer whatsoever in which we demand of God our Lord that all the sting and storm and stress and strain be pleasantly eliminated from daily existence, so that life will be a lark from morning to night. What we do, or ought to, ask in petition such as this in the Mass is merciful deliverance from what almighty God in His wisdom knows to be genuinely evil for us.

The prayer does proceed to certain particulars. First we plead: *mercifully grant peace in our days.* Perhaps it comes as a mild surprise that a petition which we of the tense thermonuclear era might have thought was the peculiar supplication of our age is actually embedded, word for word, in the ancient, established ritual of the Mass.

At the risk of appearing unduly pessimistic we must factually note that since the original sin every age of humanity has been a troubled one. Undoubtedly, one century or one decade will be more tormented than another, but such relatively slight relativity does not invalidate the bleak snafu formula: "Situation normal: all fouled up." Nevertheless, Holy Mother Church in every time and we in ours do earnestly beg God for *peace in our days* — that at least the frightful holocaust of big war may not occur.

Next we ask that *we may always be free from sin.* To this plea no qualification need be added, for in deliberate, knowing violation of divine law and the consequent estrangement from God our Father we encounter the blackest evil. There is a peace which is distinct from absence of strife between nations, and that peace, actually no less important for the individual than the other, is interior peace of mind and heart and soul. But there is only one way in which we can possess such inner tranquillity and security, and that is by being *always . . . free from sin*. Anyone who doubts this homely proposition may prove it by sad experiment.

Lastly we beg to be *safe from all trouble*. The English noun here is not precise. *Perturbation* is what the Latin says. Again, you see, Mother Church distinguishes between the external difficulties which, willy-nilly, we must meet in this valley of tears, and the interior disturbance, whether discouragement or resentment or panic or dread, which the inevitable difficulties may cause. There is simply no use and no good and no reason in asking God to spare us all trouble. It is indeed fitting to pray with the Church that we may not be excessively troubled — prostrated, overwhelmed, defeated by trouble.

Thus we pray through *Mary ever virgin, Mother of God . . . Peter and Paul and Andrew and all the saints*. In a matter as urgent as this we need all the help we can get.

44. *May the peace of the Lord be always with you. And with you, too. — May this mingling and hallowing of the body and blood of our Lord Jesus Christ avail us who receive it unto life everlasting* (prayer, in the Mass, at the Breaking of the Host).

At this point in the Mass, after the prayer for deliverance which follows the Our Father, there occurs an ancient and grave ceremony which, because of the physical situation of the moment, is not readily visible to the congregation. During

the prayer for deliverance the priest took in his right hand
the circular gold plate (the paten) which acts as a tray on
which the body of Christ may rest. He made the sign of the
cross on his own body with the paten, kissed the edge of it,
and slipped it under the consecrated host.

Now the celebrant takes the host between thumb and forefinger of both hands, breaks it cleanly down the middle, and
places the right half on the paten. He next breaks a fragment
from the lower part of the left half, placing the large re-
mainder likewise on the paten. As he says aloud, *May the
peace of the Lord be always with you,* he makes the sign
of the cross three times over the mouth of the chalice with
the small portion of the host that he is holding in the fingers
of his right hand. Finally he drops the consecrated particle
into the blood of Christ, saying softly: *May this mingling
and hallowing of the body and blood of our Lord Jesus Christ
avail us who receive it unto life everlasting.*

What is the significance of this delicate ritual?

To begin with, the fraction of the host has no historical
or immediate connection with the ill-usage and consequent
physical pain of our Savior in His Passion. Among the
Hebrews of old, bread was baked in substantial, round cakes
which were broken, at table, into individual portions. The
breaking of the bread was simply the last prelude before
actual eating, so that the phrase itself came to be equivalent
to "taking a meal." All three Evangelists who record the
institution of the Eucharist, as well as St. Paul in First Corinthians, explicitly mention the breaking of the bread before
our Lord pronounced, for the first time, the words of consecration. In the Mass, therefore, the fraction of the host is an
immediate symbolic preparation for the sacred meal which is
to follow.

Nevertheless, a more mystical symbolism here developed in the Roman rite. Says the liturgist Dom Trethowan: "The breaking of the host . . . is a relic of the practice whereby the Pope or bishop would send portions of the host consecrated by him to other priests in the neighborhood, who would place them in their own chalices as a sign of the *unity* of the Eucharist in all places."

As for the mingling of the sacred species, the action would certainly seem to derive from the earlier form of Holy Communion, still preserved in Oriental rites, whereby the faithful, as well as the priest, received our Lord under both kinds. The words *avail us who receive it unto life everlasting* bear a strong resemblance to the formula with which the Roman priest distributes Holy Communion today.

Since this ancient ceremony was followed by that impressive, significant "kiss of peace" which now is seen only in the solemn Mass, we may surely read into the ritual fraction of the host and the mingling of the body and blood of Christ a suggestion, again, of the union and fellowship that should exist between the individual members of Christ's Mystical Body. We cannot deny that it is sometimes much easier to get along with Christ than with Christians, but the Mass and the Eucharist serve always to remind us that, in the critical obligation of fraternal charity, difficulty does not mitigate or cancel out or immobilize the obligation.

Over and over again it must be explicitly observed that we who believe in Christ believe in Him together; we assist at the renewal of His death together; we receive Him in Holy Communion together. That fact may not make our neighbor in church any more appetizing; but it unquestionably, and in a powerful sense, makes him more than ever our neighbor.

45. *Lamb of God, who takest away the sins of the world, have mercy on us . . . Lamb of God, who takest away the sins of the world, grant us peace* (the *Agnus Dei* of the Mass).

In the earlier form of the Mass there occurred not only a ritual breaking of that host which the celebrant would himself receive, but the breaking into individual particles, as even today in Eastern rites, of the breads consecrated for the people. The process consumed some little time, and it is a liturgical principle to fill in such pauses with chant. What was introduced here was a litany-like acclamation by the people, at once a greeting and a plea to the Christ whom they were about to receive. At first these acclamations were prolonged throughout the breaking of the breads. Finally they took the triadic form which they have today.

Christ our Lord is now addressed in a particular manner: not as Teacher or Master or Brother or (as in the Gloria) Lord or Holy or Most High, but as the *Lamb of God.*

We think at once, of course, of John the Baptist, for it was he who first put this gentle appellation on our Lord. *Next day, John saw Jesus coming toward him; and he said: Look, this is the Lamb of God; look, this is He who takes away the sin of the world.* Again we may note that this towering and heroic John is not only mentioned, and more than once, in the Mass, but he is literally and verbatim quoted in the Mass. We really must rediscover St. John the Baptist.

Was John thinking of the Hebrew paschal lamb when he thus spoke of Christ? It could hardly have been otherwise; for an ancient Jew the inference would have been next to inevitable.

The image, therefore, is not merely one of gentleness and approachability. The paschal lamb was a victim, and the paschal lamb was a food. Once more we are reminded that the Mass is both a sacrifice and a sacrament, both a sacred immolation and a sacred eating.

Nevertheless, the appealing gentleness of the symbol of the lamb should not be overlooked, especially at this point in the Mass. We are about to receive Christ the Lord in an actual union of unique intimacy. It is with some trepidation that one might move to such a familiar meeting with *the firstborn of the risen dead, who rules over all earthly kings,* with *the Lion that comes from the tribe of Juda, from the stock of David,* with *the Lord of all lords, King of all kings.* But who will tremble or quake before a lamb, even — or especially — the *Lamb of God?*

Besides, *this is He who takes away the sin of the world.* Huge and black and foul is *the sin of the world,* the heavy guilt of all fallen and failing humanity, and of this evil my evil makes a sorry, undeniable part. Yet the power of the precious blood of this *Lamb of God* is not simply immense, it is infinite. There is no calculating the mass and the malice of human moral evil, of all the wickedness that has been and is and will be. Yet sin had a beginning, it will have an end; whereas there is no end or measure or limit to the mighty atoning achieved forever by the dear blood of Christ.

I go confidently to receive Him in the sacred eating. But that is because I keep thinking, not of me, but of Him, not of my badness, but of His goodness.

The *Agnus Dei* contains two petitions: the first, generic and repeated, for mercy; the second, for peace. One notices how the peace theme keeps recurring now, as Holy Communion approaches. Where Christ comes, there peace should be, both antecedently and consequently. The inner peace that is antecedent to Holy Communion is the fruit of a conscience that is clear of sin and cultivated attachment to sin. The peace that follows upon Holy Communion is connected with fraternal charity. *So may the peace of Christ, the very condition of your calling as members of a single body, reign in your hearts.* Thus St. Paul — and he ought to know.

46. *Lord Jesus Christ, who said to Your apostles: Peace I leave with you, My peace I give you . . .* (opening words of the set of prayers immediately before the Communion in the Mass).

The three prayers which the priest recites before receiving our Lord are of late origin, for they came into use in the sixteenth century. Moreover, these supplications are liturgically unusual, first, because they are addressed directly to our Savior rather than to the Father *through Christ our Lord,* and second, because of the use throughout of the uncommon first-person pronoun in the singular. None of this alters the fact, however, that these prayers in their context are extraordinarily appealing.

The first petition continues the theme that has been prominent ever since the Our Father, that is, throughout this sacred banquet section of the Mass. Now, though, the *peace* that is asked is more specific; it is *peace and unity* for *the Church.*

Two kinds of tranquillity the Church must always strive and pray for: freedom from external persecution and freedom from internal division. It is hard to say which of these two dangers is more menacing to the well-being of the Bride of Christ. While she is being attacked and tormented externally, she cannot really be herself. When she is torn asunder interiorly, she is not really herself.

We understand, though with a kind of wonder, how those of heterodox persuasion sincerely seem to find positive virtue and even the hand of God in doctrinal variety and situational morality, but we keep hearing Christ say to His Father in His exalted sacerdotal prayer: *And I have given them the privilege which Thou gavest to Me, that they should all be one, as We are one; that while Thou art in Me, I may be in them, and so they may be perfectly made one.*

The second of these eloquent prayers is an act of contrition. It asks the Eucharistic Christ for deliverance *from all my sins and from every evil;* it begs that he who prays *may always cling to Your commandments and never be separated from You.* Here again we hear a clear echo of our Savior's sublime discourse at the Last Supper: *If a man has any love for Me, he will be true to My word* (that is, as is said later, *keep My commandments*); *and then he will win My Father's love, and We will both come to him, and make our continual abode with him.* Holy Communion, then, is not simply physical union even of the highest order; it implies and involves a union of wills that will long outlast the corporal, sacramental union.

At the last, the priest seems to recall for one terribly sobering moment the solemn warning issued by St. Paul: *And therefore, if anyone eats this bread or drinks this cup of the Lord unworthily, he will be held to account for the Lord's body and blood . . . he is eating and drinking damnation to himself if he eats and drinks unworthily. . . .* So, at the final moment before he receives Christ, the priest begs that this Communion may not mean for him *judgment and condemnation,* but may be *protection of mind and body and* a sovereign *remedy.*

All is now done that with God's help and the sure guidance of the Church can be humanly done. Striking his breast, the

priest thrice utters the humble cry of the army officer in the
Gospel and takes in the anointed fingers of his right hand
the two halves of the consecrated host. With them he makes
the sign of the cross. Then, saying simply: *May the body of
our Lord Jesus Christ keep my soul unto life everlasting,* he
bows down and receives his Lord.

Into what then transpires between priest and High Priest,
between man and God, between Christ and the other Christ,
no man will inquire. The priest would be the first to say that
he is in no sense up to or capable of or competent for the
level of this union and this communication. But the fact
stands. The two Christs are now one.

47.   *What return shall I make to the Lord for all He has
given me? I will take the cup of salvation, and I will call upon
the name of the Lord* (words spoken softly by the celebrant
of the Mass before he consumes the blood of Christ).

As we know well, the Lord Christ is completely and vitally
present under each species in the Eucharistic mystery. Hence,
after receiving Christ in the host, the priest at Mass is directed
to pause briefly in adoration. For this reverential act the
Church puts no words on the priest's lips. He will speak to
his Lord as the Holy Spirit gives him to speak and according
to the inmost reality of what he most truly and deeply *is.* His
meditation, however, will be short, for the ritual action,
which always takes precedence over private devotion, must
not be interrupted. Proceeding, then, to complete the sacrificial meal, the celebrant quietly pronounces the question
and answer which form our present text. In the Latin the first
phrase is: *Quid retribuam, What shall I give back?*

The Christian problem of gratitude is one of the several questions which come to a sharp point in the Mass.

There can be no doubt, of course, about our very real obligation of gratitude as we face almighty God. If our first duty toward the Supreme Being and divine Majesty is to adore Him, the second, scarcely distinguishable from the first, is to thank Him. We are in debt to God for everything, simply. *After all, friend,* says St. Paul to his typical, confident Corinthian, *who is it that gives thee this pre-eminence? What powers hast thou, that did not come to thee by gift? And if they came to thee by gift, why dost thou boast of them* — or, we might add, take them for granted — *as if there were no gift in question?*

But mere words, when we set about being grateful to God, are so inadequate. Not that the formal expression of gratitude is ever to be despised, as we see from this and many other places in the Church's liturgy. Still, words do not really prove anything, do they? Talk is disturbingly cheap. The Christian, therefore, will feel the need of implementing his inner thankfulness to the extravagantly generous Lord of all who has been so good to him.

Gratitude ought to be an attitude. That is to say, a religious man's habitual outlook and viewpoint and general manner ought to be colored and influenced, if it will not be dominated, by an explicit sense of thankfulness.

There is a kind of man who is satisfied with nothing. Existent reality does not live up to this individual's expectations. Things are all wrong, and that's the long and short of it — the weather, the season, the price of things, the digestion, the nerves, the national situation, the international pandemonium, the state of education, the doings of the Church, the antics of people. People. They get the awful prize, whatever it is. People, as a modern philosopher has observed succinctly but surely not without satisfaction, are hell.

Now the difficulty with all this is that it is true. Does it come as any surprise to a Christian to hear for the thousandth time that original sin did make a botch of God's good creation? In other words, if I insist on being a connoisseur of trouble, I will indeed be a connoisseur. If I am determined to find fault, there will always be plenty of fault to find. If I will not cheer up, then I must expect to droop down.

We will not trouble now to point out that there really is another and brighter side to this poor old world, fallen and fallible as it is. Our present interest lies not in any external situation but in an interior attitude. No doubt some of us must carry through life, like a cross (for it is no less), a temperament that is darker and more captious than most. But temperament, while it explains, does not altogether excuse. I may be dyspeptic to my ears — so to speak — but I am still not quit of my obligation of gratitude toward God.

What we are trying to say is that a splendid form of gratitude to God is cultivated cheerfulness toward men.

48.   *May the body of our Lord Jesus Christ keep your soul unto life everlasting* (words spoken by the priest as he gives Holy Communion to each individual).

As soon as the celebrant of the Mass has completed his Communion, the people of God — *plebs Tua sancta: Your holy people* — come forward to receive their Eucharistic Lord, to share in the heavenly banquet. Again it must be urged that the sacred eating is the normal, integral culmination of the sacred sacrifice.

What shall we say about Holy Communion? Above all else and as its name declares, Communion is a union. Christ is a Person, I am a person, and these persons are brought together in the reception of the Eucharist. They do not merely meet; they do not simply note or acknowlege or come into proximity with one another; nor are they mingled or blended or fused so that one is actually pre-empted, as it were, and ceases to exist by reason of the overpowering existence of the other. Only one word will serve for this holy event: in Communion Christ and the one who receives Christ are united — literally, factually, and completely united. In this coming together no damage whatever is done to either the *I* or the *You,* for this *I-You* union is altogether respectful. Indeed, it is loving.

That important word, which we employ so readily and even sincerely, immediately provokes a question. When we say that Holy Communion is a loving coming together, do we imply that the reception of this sacrament is a fond and tender experience? We do not so imply. Some exposition is in order here.

It is perfectly natural that we all think of love as something that is experienced and something that is delightful to experience. The most rabid realist can no more really renounce all romance than a writer not of the first rank can keep clear of alluring alliteration. But the idea of love as warmth and tenderness must simply be disciplined, if not rejected, when we begin to examine the relationship between God and man. No one is going to contend that man cannot feel tenderness toward God; he can and occasionally does. What must be insisted upon is (*a*) that ordinarily and for the most part the average, normal, and completely earnest man of faith does not *in fact* feel such warmth toward God, and (*b*) that such lack is positively inconsequential.

To state the entire large matter in large terms, religion, in the Catholic view, is not primarily an experience. It is believing and doing.

If people persist in feeling disappointment because their Communions are not more moving occasions, then they are going to be disappointed, and there's an end. Judging from the evidence of our Savior's life on earth, we may presume that God's major problem and prime, practical objective in dealing with us who believe in Him is effectively to prevail on us to live on a supernatural rather than on a natural level. Supernatural love is only analogous to natural love: they are alike, except where they are very different. And if anyone wishes a single clue to the decisive difference between them, it may be sought in a word which we have just used. We do not say that this is the whole story or that no qualification need be added, but we venture to offer one thumping simplification. Where natural love will be affective, supernatural love will be effective.

Our dealings with Christ in Holy Communion will be reflective and volitional; at times they will be laborious. What is important is not the ease of our discussions with our exalted Guest and Friend, but the subjects that are raised and the determinations that are reached. It might be possible upon occasion (the psychology of the moment may be favorable) to give to Christ in Holy Communion a rousing and most affectionate welcome. Splendid. But we may be sure that He who has come to us is only waiting for us to pause and give Him a chance to say something. He will then say quietly: *The*

*man who loves Me is the man who keeps the commandments
he has from Me.*

It is fitting that we prolong our discussion of the people's
Communion in the Mass. We wish now to turn our attention to
the matter of the effects or benefits of Holy Communion.
What does this sacramental reception do for us?

At first sight the question itself might seem presumptuous,
almost impudent. If, in sacramental Communion, we are actually, personally united with Christ, the Son of God and
Savior of the world, what more in the world could we possibly
expect or desire? The reason why the theologians unhesitatingly describe the Eucharist as the greatest of the sacraments is that in all the other sacraments we receive grace,
but in Holy Communion we receive the fount and source and
author of grace. Nevertheless, since both theology and the
liturgy (which is theology in ritual act) discuss the effects of
Holy Communion, let us do so here.

According to one liturgical prayer, in the reception of the
Eucharist *the soul is filled with grace.* Now we must immediately remind ourselves that the accession of grace is
never *felt;* as a distinguished contemporary theologian has expressed it, grace does not operate on the level of the senses.
We are not to confuse the strictly supernatural reality that is
grace with the psychological sense of relief or restoration or
well-being that, for example, may or may not follow a contrite confession.

Perhaps the most concrete form which the grace of the
Eucharist takes is strength or fortitude. But again, this en-
ergizing of the soul does not commonly reveal itself and
certainly does not make itself felt at the moment of the Communion. The new fortitude which the soul has acquired will or

should be manifest in the hours which follow. In short, the person who, on a given day, has received Holy Communion will be better able to cope with the issues of that day than the person who has not so received. No doubt there are those to whom this proposition does not appear empirically warranted. There are many more who could and would swear to it.

Another effect of the Eucharist, and one which is stressed by every authority, is an intensification of fraternal charity.

The Eucharist does not immediately simplify the problem of Christian charity by wonderfully making our neighbor a much more agreeable and amiable fellow. One of our most persistent religious errors is to look naïvely for the effects of prayer and the sacraments in the world about us rather than in ourselves. My Holy Communion will not even slightly sweeten the sour disposition of my boss or of the fishwife who lives next door. What my Communion could do and ought to do, at least in degree and gradually, is miraculously and against all reason to pacify and control me in my necessary dealings with the boss and the fishwife.

At any rate, the earnest Catholic will profit considerably by adverting with explicitness to this social aspect of his Holy Communion. Over and over again we must remind ourselves that we all receive our Lord *together,* and that such community of sacred action must not remain a purely external or circumstantial thing. No one will ever pretend that it will ever be easy — though the saints, to our embarrassment, made it look easy — to get along perfectly or even quietly with the pests and screwballs and dimwits and barbarians of this world. But at least we can, in Holy Communion, consciously, deliberately renounce all bitterness and hostility; we can resolve again to be kinder and more patient today; we can sincerely commend to God in Christ, even if it takes a little time, all the pests, screwballs, dimwits, and barbarians of our rich and varied acquaintance. Let us be so grateful, faithful reader, that you and I are not pests, etc.

A further effect of Holy Communion need only be mentioned, for we have previously taken note of this consoling truth. The Eucharist is *pignus vitae aeternae, a pledge of eternal life*. The union between the soul in bliss and the Triune God is not different in essence from the Eucharistic union between the soul and the Lord Christ. In that radical sense every Communion is the inception of heaven and hence a new promise that someday the union which is now veiled and of faith will be complete, ecstatic, and beatific. With deep significance we say with St. John in our Holy Communion: *Come, Lord Jesus*.

49. *Grant, Lord, that what we have taken with our lips we may receive with a pure mind. . . . May Your body, Lord, which I have received and Your blood which I have drunk cleave to my inmost parts. . . .* (thanksgiving prayers recited by the priest immediately after the Communion of the Mass).

With the Communion of the Faithful the sacred action of the Mass is essentially complete. However, as is the case whenever civilized people take food, there is tidying up to be done. In the technical term, the priest now "purifies" the chalice. Lest any least residue of the blood of Christ remain, the celebrant of the Mass rinses the chalice, first with a little wine, then with a few drops of wine in a larger quantity of water, both of which "ablutions" he consumes. Finally, he dries the chalice with the bit of linen that for this reason is called the "purificator." During all this the Church puts upon the lips of the priest two short and simple prayers of thanksgiving.

The first of these calm supplications voices one of those double contrasts which are so often found in liturgical prayer. Contrast is one of the most natural and effective of artistic and pedagogical devices, and someday someone is going to write a splendid essay on Mother Church's employment of antithesis.

The two sets of contraries in the present passage are the familiar ones. The external sacramental sign or physical act (*what we have taken with our lips*) is set over against the interior, invisible, sacramental effect (*we may receive with a pure mind*); and, as always, the significant but ephemeral moment (*the temporal gift*) is matched with the ultimate goal (*an eternal remedy*). Always, always does Mother Church lead us from the material to the supernatural, from time to eternity.

Even the Mass, with all its unutterable sublimity, is a sign, and signs, as their name signifies and St. Paul asserts, shall pass away. *The time will come when we shall outgrow prophecy, when speaking with tongues will come to an end, when* [imperfect] *knowledge will be swept away. . . . At present —* and, if we may boldly add to St. Paul, even in the present holiness that is the Mass — *we are looking at a confused reflection in a mirror; then, we shall see face to face. . . .*

The second thanksgiving prayer likewise gives us a pair, but the members now stand in combination rather than in contrast: *that in me there may remain no stain of evil, for Your pure and holy sacraments have refreshed me.* The Church again underscores two of the effects of the Eucharist, interior purification and that inner strengthening which is refreshment and restoration.

In certain matters both of faith and practical piety we must be willing to run the risk of overemphasis and tiresome repetition. Thus we have to remind ourselves steadily, as we think about the wondrous effects of the Eucharist, that these effects, being supernatural in character, are not ordinarily *felt* by the recipient.

It is pathetically difficult for us creatures of flesh and blood and sensation to go on being fully convinced of what lies beyond the reach of our sensory and emotional perceptions. Perhaps the best way, except that it is the worst way, of discovering what Mass and Holy Communion really do for us would be to stay away from them.

The Catholic who is in good conscience may periodically wonder whether, after all, the sacraments actually count for much in his life. But it is as instructive as it is painful to see how the Catholic who is barred from the Eucharist longs for the Eucharist. There are cases, of course, where this longing does not exist. But those poor souls never did have any sense of the supernatural, because they never did have any but a mechanical and most feeble faith.

We need not go to such extremes, however, in order to be sure that Catholic people not only believe in the Mass and Holy Communion, but are altogether convinced of the rich and realistic benefits of both. Not many hours before these deathless lines were committed to paper, the writer was happily distracted as he celebrated Mass at the side altar in a city church. He was distracted, if that be the correct word, as line after line after line of men, women, and children received our Lord at the Communion rail. The day was a weekday. The hour was uncomfortably early. The weather was inclement. *Q. E. D.*

Christ's good people *know* that the Eucharist does all that the Church says it does.

50. *Grant us, we pray, almighty God, that we who receive from You the grace of a new life may always glory in Your gift* (Postcommunion of the Mass for the Second Sunday after Easter).

When, after the Communion, the ablutional tidying-up is completed, the celebrant of the Mass moves to his right and reads from the missal the brief Communion Verse. Exactly as at the Offertory, this short saying is a relic — in this case, a relic of the psalm which the people used to sing during the Communion Procession. One realizes, as he studies the liturgy, how much *physical* participation there was on the part of the laity as they shared in the sacrificial action.

Pausing only to kiss the altar and greet the people once more, the priest directly reads the final prayer of the Mass, the Postcommunion. Says the liturgist Dom Trethowan: "The Postcommunion Prayer sums up in the manner of the Secret, using the same terse and luminous language, the significance of the great act which has been performed."

By way of illustration, let us examine the Postcommunion of the Mass for the Second Sunday after Easter. The key words in this prayer are *the grace of a new life*. The Latin uses a very active word, for it speaks of a *vivification*.

Sometimes we who believe in and honestly try to love our Lord seem to be attentive to what everyone except our Lord says about the Eucharist. But let the kindly reader take up his New Testament and read carefully, in the sixth chapter of St. John's Gospel, the six verses from 54 to 59, which contain our Savior's only specific remarks on the effects of eating and drinking His body and blood. In this short passage some form of the word *live* occurs seven times, more than once to a verse. Christ's own insistence, then, in connection with the Eucharist, is that the Eucharist is life-giving, vivifying.

This life, which is actually imparted in baptism and nourished by Holy Communion, has three aspects.

First, as is evident, the life in question is not physical and natural, but spiritual and supernatural. Christ promises this life to *the man who eats My flesh and drinks My blood.* But eating and drinking are vital acts, and there is no point in promising physical life to anyone thus physically alive. A little later our Lord on that same occasion said carefully to the shocked crowd: *Only the spirit gives life; the flesh is of no avail; and the words I have been speaking to you are spirit, and life.* Now supernatural life consists essentially in the possession of sanctifying grace. The Eucharist does not ordinarily convey sanctifying grace where it is absent. The one who receives Holy Communion must be already alive not only physically but spiritually, and Christ in the sacrament will then powerfully nourish that supernatural life.

Next, this life is literally an extension of, or, much better, an actual sharing in, the interior life of Christ. *As I live because of the Father, the living Father who has sent Me, so he who eats Me will live, in his turn, because of Me.* The parallelism between the inner life of Christ, and the inner life of him who Eucharistically receives Christ could not be more clearly or more strongly expressed. One thinks immediately of the celebrated cry of St. Paul, that perfect echo, as we might expect, of what our Lord had said: *With Christ I hang upon the cross, and yet I am alive; or rather, not I; it is Christ that lives in me.* Perhaps, as we move in life from hour to hour, we do not advert nearly often enough to the startling fact that we are living with a life distinct from our

own, a life incalculably superior to our own, a life that is no
other than the Christ-life. Such is the exalted existence that
people throw away by committing serious sin.

Lastly, this *new life* is nothing less than everlasting, and such
is the special point of insistence in our Savior's own exposition.
*The man who eats My flesh and drinks My blood enjoys
eternal life, and I will raise him up* — physical death is therefore supposed — *at the last day . . . the man who eats this
bread will live eternally.* It is heartening to reflect that every
Mass and especially every Holy Communion is a concrete, living pledge from Christ in Person that someday,
somehow, all will be well with us. Not only well, but perfectly well, and entirely, everlastingly perfect.

We ask, as the prayer closes, that we *may always glory in
Your gift;* the gift of the Mass, the gift of the Eucharist, the
gift (for it is only a matter of time, then) of *eternal life.* It is
really wonderful to pray as the Church prays.

51. *Go, you are dismissed. Thanks be to God. May the
homage of my service be pleasing to You, Holy Trinity. . . .
May almighty God bless you, Father, Son, and Holy Spirit*
(concluding words of the Mass).

At the end of the Postcommunion Prayer the priest closes the
Mass book, and the little gesture seems significant in so many
ways. The holy action is completed. The Lord has passed; He
has come and gone. The time of praying is over; the time of
doing is at hand. The priest at the altar may experience a
slight inward sigh: he has just so many Masses to say in his
life, and now the precious sum is smaller by one. He moves
to the center of the altar, kisses the altar table, and again

greets the people. He then pronounces the words of dismissal.

There is an interesting formula at the beginning of the liturgy for a priestly ordination. At the very outset all who are involved are ritually warned that none shall depart until the Mass is concluded and the apostolic blessing received. In an ordination there would, of course, be special reason for such a caution, yet Catholics ought to be aware of the general truth that is implied. On the most solemn and significant human occasions people do not dash in and out according to individual whim. If they are civilized and possess any concept of occasion, they come to a large event when they are summoned and they depart when they are given leave. If this simple truth of social behavior has become obscured in our day, it can only be concluded that we are less civilized than our grandfathers, less perceptive of significance, less disciplined and mannerly in our ways. Perhaps we suffer in this regard from one of the multiple effects of double-feature movies, to which people come at any loose moment and escape when the tedium can no longer be borne.

The intelligent Catholic at Mass will not depart until he has religiously answered, either with the community or the altar boy, *Thanks be to God* to the priest's courteous words of dismissal, and has received the kindly, priestly blessing.

The celebrant of the Mass now bends over the altar for the last time, and for the last time asks fulfillment of the double, most general, intent of the Mass: that God be honored and man be helped. He then turns to the kneeling people and blesses them in the consecrated Trinitarian formula. Various things have been blessed often in the course of the Mass. Now, at the end, the blessing of God is bestowed, by him who has such enviable power, on the devoted and beloved folk of God.

The Mass is ended. The sacrifice of Calvary has been re-newed; God has been fittingly worshiped; the faithful have been purified, refreshed, consoled, uplifted, immeasurably strengthened. Now begins the test of the Holy Sacrifice. Now the Mass is put to the proof.

Time and again — for so it must be — our Catholic people have been warned that they must not lead departmentalized lives. It is true that daily life is inevitably departmentalized in the rudimentary sense that a man cannot be doing this when he is actually doing that. A man sleeps and then wakes; he works and afterward plays; he feeds his body and in another hour he feeds his mind. But it is always the same man who does all this. And just as he will be influenced (not to say, ruled) by the same temperament and psychology no matter what he may be doing at any given moment, so the Catholic man will presumably be influenced (not to say, ruled) by the same spirituality in the whole range of his categorized activities.

Anyone coming from Mass and Holy Communion is fully alive with the inner life of Christ Himself. But that life, which involves a whole interior attitude or posture or out-look, must at once enter into competition with all the other lives a man must lead: physical life, the life of the senses, the life of work and business and acquisition, the inner, active life of the mind, family life, social life. In every one of these numberless daily competitions, something has got to give. In each instance and almost in each instant, the Christ-life now being lived by Christ's member must either best the competition or be worsted by it. It's a difficult situation, but one which ought daily to improve in favor of the Christ-life and not, as the diplomats say automatically these days, deteriorate.

52. *The Lord be with you. And with you, too. The beginning of the holy Gospel according to St. John. Glory to You, Lord. At the beginning of time the Word already was . . .* (the last Gospel in the Mass).

The prologue of St. John's Gospel is without parallel in the four Gospels; perhaps it is without parallel in human communication. It is theology; it is poetry; it is mystery. Commentators without number have expounded this sublime utterance, and always the reader comes away feeling that the utterance has not been expounded. Small wonder that this prologue began to have, in simple but seeing Christian eyes, the value of a sacramental. These 14 scriptural verses were read aloud to ward off evil; they were read as a prayer for fair weather; they are read even today over the sick. Small wonder that in the Middle Ages this prologue became an epilogue — an epilogue to the Mass.

There seem to be three steps or successive ideas in the Johannine prologue: the divinity of Christ, the herald of Christ, the coming of Christ.

St. John proclaims the divinity of our Lord in three clipped, massive statements by which are asserted the preexistence of Christ before creation, His coexistence with God, His identity with God. *And the Word was God.* Christ is both Creator and the instrument whereby creation came to be. Then, using the two symbols that will govern his whole Gospel, John declares that Christ is *life* and that Christ is *light*.

Even in St. Paul there is no Christological pronouncement that can match these first five verses in the fourth Gospel. It may be that here human expression has come closest to uttering the unutterable.

Next, John the Evangelist turns abruptly to John the

Baptist. No doubt this passage is polemical. Even yet a band of tenacious disciples or inheritors of the Baptist's movement were carrying a messianic torch for that poor, innocent John who could not have disclaimed messiaship more emphatically than he did. John the Evangelist, in his turn, could not be more explicit on the question: *He* (the Baptist) *was not the Light; he was sent to bear witness to the Light.*

Apart, however, from all polemical intent, the person and function of the precursor serve the Evangelist as a fitting transition to the climactic subject of the prologue, the coming among us of the divine Word.

How is it possible to comment on the lines that follow? *He, through whom the world was made, was in the world, and the world treated Him as a stranger. He came to what was His own, and they who were His own gave Him no welcome.* Each one of us must say here what he must say.

All is not lost, however; far from it. *But all those who did welcome Him He empowered to become the children of God.* . . . Let us look steadily and as if for the first time at that wondrous expression, *the children of God.* St. Paul says the same: *The Spirit Himself thus assures our spirit, that we are children of God; and if we are His children, then we are His heirs, too; heirs of God, sharing the inheritance of Christ.* . . .

In order to attain to such splendor all I must do is *welcome* Him whom God has sent. I must therefore seriously consider what it means, in very deed, to *welcome* Christ.

And the Word was made flesh, and came to dwell among us; and we had sight of His glory, glory such as belongs to the Father's only-begotten Son, full of grace and truth.

It is a marvel, extravagant as the suggestion may seem, that we all do not come from Mass in a sort of devout daze, repeating inwardly snatches of what we have just heard: . . .

flesh . . . dwell among us . . . sight of His glory . . . only-begotten Son . . . full of grace and truth. . . . If Catholics do not deeply love Christ in God and God in Christ, it is not the fault of the Holy Spirit breathing in the Catholic liturgy.

We rise and genuflect and quietly file out of God's house. It is good that we came here, stood on Calvary, assisted at Mass, received Christ as our food. We came in sore need. We turn away replete, *full of grace and truth.*

Deo gratias. Thanks be to God.